LOVE SIGNS

Elaine Dawn

ADAMS MEDIA
NEW YORK LONDON TORONTO SYDNEY NEW DELHI

adamsmedia
Adams Media
An Imprint of Simon & Schuster, Inc.
57 Littlefield Street
Avon, Massachusetts 02322

First Adams Media hardcover edition May 2019

ADAMS MEDIA and colophon are trademarks of Simon & Schuster.

For information about special discounts for bulk purchases, please contact Simon & Schuster Special Sales at 1-866-506-1949 or business@simonandschuster.com.

The Simon & Schuster Speakers Bureau can bring authors to your live event. For more information or to book an event contact the Simon & Schuster Speakers Bureau at 1-866-248-3049 or visit our website at www.simonspeakers.com.

Interior design by Michelle Kelly
Interior images © Getty Images/MicrovOne

Manufactured in the United States of America

10 9 8 7 6 5 4 3 2 1

Library of Congress Cataloging-in-Publication Data
Names: Dawn, Elaine, author.
Title: Love signs / Elaine Dawn.
Description: Avon, Massachusetts: Adams Media, 2019.
Identifiers: LCCN 2018031892 (print) | LCCN 2018040821 (ebook) | ISBN 9781507209509 (hc) | ISBN 9781507209516 (ebook)
Subjects: LCSH: Astrology. | Love--Miscellanea. | Mate selection--Miscellanea.
Classification: LCC BF1729.L6 (ebook) | LCC BF1729.L6 K674 2018 (print) | DDC 133.5--dc23
LC record available at https://lccn.loc.gov/2018031892

ISBN 978-1-5072-0950-9
ISBN 978-1-5072-0951-6 (ebook)

Contents

Introduction

Love—exciting and inspiring, complicated and challenging—is filled with amazing moments and confusion; passion and heartache; and, most of all, *plenty* of trial and error. Maybe you go on a first date and the connection is intoxicating, but you never hear back from them. Or maybe you and your partner of many years have been struggling to communicate with each other lately. You may be left wondering sometimes if love is really worth it. But what if there was a way to peer into the psyche of that partner or crush—to see what it is they are truly looking for in love? Better yet, what if you could further understand what *you* need in a partner? That would be impossible...right? Actually, you are holding the key to unlocking the mysteries of romantic compatibility: astrology! By understanding someone's Sun sign, you can figure out *exactly* how they flirt, date, and approach long-term partnership.

In *Love Signs*, you'll discover everything you need to know about how each astrological sign acts in love and what they desire in a romantic relationship. From the dos and don'ts of initial attraction to the creation of lasting love, each sign has unique values and ways of operating when it comes to romance. As you explore your love matches, keep in mind that a sign relationship that may look troubling on paper can flourish given time and care. Your Sun sign only tells part of the story, so if you find yourself falling for (or in love with) someone who isn't listed as a potential love match, trust your gut.

As you read, you'll also notice each sign has a few recurring aspects. A sign has a gender (male or female) and an element (fire, earth, air, or water). The fire and air signs are considered male, and the water and earth signs are considered female. Fire signs are passionate and vivacious, earth signs are practical and stable, air signs are intellectual and social, and water signs are intuitive and emotional. In addition to its element, each sign is classified as one of three qualities: cardinal, fixed, or mutable. Cardinal signs kick off each new season and promote action. Fixed signs occur in the height of each season and maintain movement. Mutable signs signal the change of one season to the next and excel at change and transformation. Finally, each sign is ruled by a planet that exemplifies the characteristics of that sign.

The two planets that most concern love are Venus and Mars. Venus, or Aphrodite in ancient Greek mythology, was the goddess of beauty and love. Mars, or Ares, was the god of war. Everyone has Venus and Mars located in a sign in their astrological chart, and the placement of these planets will describe the feminine yin and masculine yang, or receptive and assertive, dynamic in their lives. The placement of Venus and Mars has nothing to do with traditional gender roles, however, as a man can exhibit yin (receptive) qualities, and a woman can exhibit yang (assertive) qualities.

Regardless of who you are, the truth is that love can be quite scary: it's not easy opening up your heart for the world to see! But by deepening your understanding of astrology, you will gain invaluable insights to make falling (and staying) in love a little less complicated. So, go ahead and set the mood: light a few candles and put out the good china. It's time to let the stars guide you to love.

Love Signs Compatibility Quiz

The following compatibility quiz will reveal truths about you and your current partner, crush, or potential future love interests. When you're finished, tally up your score to discover which Sun signs perfectly match your zodiac love style. But remember, love is complex: only you can truly understand the nooks and crannies of your heart, so if you find yourself drawn to someone who isn't within your list of potential matches, trust your instincts. Go ahead, dig in!

1. **You meet someone new—someone you really like. If this potential partner went digging into your past, what would you be most worried about them discovering?**
   a Family secrets
   b Former lifestyle choices
   c Specific ex-partners
   d Past infidelity

2. **After having the best first date of your life, what do you do?**

   a Dream in Technicolor and obsess relentlessly until the next time you meet up
   b Gush about your romance on social media—the world needs to know
   c Tell only your closest companion—you don't want to get too excited
   d Go on a date with someone else; you never put all of your eggs in one basket

3. **With the right person, you're a sucker for:**

   a Sincere words of affection
   b A delicious, home-cooked dinner
   c Physical intimacy, including cuddling, holding hands, and kissing
   d Shared bank accounts, stock options, and a diversified portfolio

4. **Your partner tells you an extremely juicy secret about a mutual friend and asks you not to tell anyone else. What do you do?**

   a Take it to the grave
   b Start yapping—you can't help it
   c Tell a trusted confidant, such as your mother or sibling
   d Share it with your friends, but make them promise not to tell your partner you spilled the beans

5. **In your longest relationship, how did you relate to each other?**

   a You were completely alike—practically mirror images of each other
   b You were complete opposites, but you balanced each other out
   c Your private relationship was very different than it appeared to the public
   d It was love—but it felt a bit flat

6. **What was the fastest you ever fell in love?**

   a One day—total love at first sight
   b Between one and two months
   c After several months—you needed to build trust
   d You felt it from the beginning, but it took you quite a long time to admit it

7. **What do you do when you're stuck in horrible traffic?**

   a Crank up the tunes to shut out the chaos
   b Distract yourself by fixing your hair or makeup in the mirror
   c Curse under your breath—your mood is quickly going south
   d Go to full-on road rage—you didn't even *know* you could get that angry

8. **What is the one thing you couldn't live without in a partner?**

   a Charisma
   b Great sense of style
   c Physical intimacy
   d Financial security

9. **Do you believe in magic?**

   a Yes—you own something that brings you good luck and check your horoscope from time to time
   b A bit—you're open-minded but aren't fully invested in any particular belief
   c Extremely—you've cast spells by bathing in enchanted herbs, blended love potions, and always follow the lunar cycles
   d Nope—not at all

10. **What would you most likely do before saying "I do"?**

   a Organize a massive event, getting into full wedding-zilla mode
   b Elope—after all, this is about you two, not anyone else
   c Make sure the in-laws and extended family don't get in the way too much
   d Have a prenup signed by both you and your betrothed

11. **After dating someone for a month, you accidentally stumble upon a porn search on their computer. What do you do?**

   a Laugh and shrug it off
   b Suggest you watch one of the videos together
   c Wait a few days, and then casually mention pornography to see if your boo will bring it up without prodding
   d Freak out and go into full crisis mode

12. **What type of mate turns you on?**

   a An intellectual wiseass—humor is everything
   b An out-of-the-box nonconformist
   c A worldly, spiritual soul with an artistic vision
   d A "tell it like it is, no matter how much it may hurt" person

13. **You're at a party. Your boo of two months is spending the entire night with an ex instead of you. What's the worst you're capable of doing in retaliation?**

   a Leaving without saying goodbye
   b Confronting your mate in public and demanding to not be ignored
   c Flirting with the most attractive person in the room
   d Waiting until after you have left the party to have a private confrontation
   e Something a bit crazy

14. **Who would you be more likely to have casual sex with?**

    a An attractive good friend
    b A sexy stranger
    c An ex-lover
    d A dangerously unavailable crush

15. **In most situations, you're *not* likely to say:**

    a I cannot
    b I will not
    c I do not
    d I should not

16. **What do you do if your dinner date is rude to the server?**

    a Defend the server
    b Make a joke to lighten the mood
    c Lose respect for your date entirely—check, please
    d Calmly explain why you don't like that behavior

17. **What first attracts you to a potential mate?**

    a A dazzling smile
    b Style
    c Physique
    d Social finesse

18. **You're on a third date with a person you really like; however, now your date is flirting shamelessly with the bartender. What do you do?**

 a Decide to never see that date again
 b Hope it's just a one-time thing

19. **After a heated argument, your partner of four months unexpectedly breaks up with you and leaves. What do you do?**

 a Wait for them to contact you—you are too proud to beg
 b Scream, kick or throw things, cry, or yell
 c Accept their decision—it clearly wouldn't have worked long term
 d Reach out once your partner has cooled off and try to smooth things over

20. **How do you feel about participating in some major PDA (public displays of affection)?**

 a It's fun occasionally, but only when you're really in the mood
 b You're obsessed with voyeurism—the idea of people watching really turns you on
 c If your partner is into it, maybe, but it's not really your thing
 d No way! Displays of affection should be private, *not* public

21. **What do you do to relax after a stressful day?**

a Watch a favorite movie in your pajamas, with a pint of ice cream

b Switch your phone to airplane mode, and shut out the world

c Seek an orgasm—by any means necessary

d Chat with your friends and browse social media—you're always curious about the latest gossip

22. **Which best describes your role in a relationship?**

a A partner: you love to be paired

b A free spirit: you're fiercely independent

c A giver: you're willing to sacrifice a lot for the ones you love

d A doer: you love to problem-solve

23. **What would you most likely do on a day off?**

a Enjoy a luxurious meal at your favorite restaurant

b Go to the movies

c Dive into a really great book

d Go on a spontaneous adventure

24. **What turns you on professionally?**

a Creativity

b Stability

c Philanthropy

d Power

e None of these options—career pursuits are irrelevant

25. It's easy for you to fall in "like" when someone is...

a Clever, with the gift of gab
b Extremely physically attractive
c Passionate about their hobbies and interests
d Well-off...and not afraid to spend their money

26. Your friend wants to set you up on a date. How do you approach the situation?

a First talk on the phone—if there's no chemistry, I'm not wasting my time
b Make a plan for dinner and drinks—you love the excitement
c Poke around on social media to find out as much info as you can before meeting IRL (in real life)
d Meet for coffee—after all, even if there aren't any romantic sparks, maybe you can make a new friend

27. When faced with a difficult decision in life, you typically:

a Ask everyone you know for advice
b Flip a coin
c Trust your gut
d Make an extensive pro and con list; you want to weigh all your options

28. Which of these is a deal breaker for a long-term partnership?

a Constant restlessness and hyperactivity
b Lack of motivation
c Extreme people-pleasing
d Excessive arguing

29. After a serious heartbreak, how long does it take for you to move on?

a Years. It's very hard for you to let go
b You rebound quickly, but usually it just prolongs the pain
c Until you meet your next partner
d It varies based on circumstance

30. You're on a first date, and the chemistry is really intense. What are you thinking?

a Is this "the one"?
b The sex better be great.
c Who will make the first move?
d This is too perfect—what are they hiding?

31. Which quality do you find most intriguing in another person?

a Danger
b Eccentricity
c Stability
d Sarcasm

32. **After a crazy night, you wake up in your new flame's bed. The morning sun is shining brightly, and your lover says you look great in the daylight. How do you respond?**

a You say "thank you," because you know it's true
b You say "thank you," but worry they're just being nice—you definitely need to shower
c You say "thank you," and return the compliment
d You turn away—you hate compliments

33. **What makes you laugh?**

a Ironic, witty, and clever situational humor
b Slapstick—people tripping over things really makes you giggle
c Characters and larger-than-life personalities
d Teasing—you love playful taunts

34. **When it comes to dating, your best friend would say your greatest flaw is:**

a Impulsivity
b Clinginess
c Immaturity
d Pickiness

35. **Your new partner comes home visibly intoxicated after a night of hanging out with friends. How do you react?**

a Assume the worst; they were definitely on their worst behavior

b Get them water, help them change clothes, and tuck them into bed
c Amuse yourself by asking playful questions about their evening
d Ignore them; you were already asleep

Scoring

a = 1 point b = 2 points c = 3 points d = 4 points

Question 13

e = subtract 4 points

Question 18

a = 10 points b = 3 points

Question 24

a = 10 points b = 1 point c = 10 points
d = 10 points e = 10 points

Question 35

a = subtract 3 points b = subtract 10 points
c = 4 points d = 15 points

Now, add up your points, and find your own Sun sign in the following table (the left column). Based on your score, these are the signs you best match with romantically.

Most Compatible Signs

Zodiac Sign	Score: 21–85	Score: 86–163
Aries	Aries, Cancer, Scorpio, Leo	Aquarius, Scorpio, Cancer, Pisces, Leo
Taurus	Gemini, Aquarius, Scorpio	Scorpio, Virgo, Aquarius, Gemini
Gemini	Gemini, Aquarius, Leo, Taurus	Gemini, Taurus, Virgo
Cancer	Scorpio, Leo, Aries, Pisces	Leo, Scorpio, Pisces
Leo	Gemini, Sagittarius, Cancer, Scorpio, Leo	Sagittarius, Gemini, Aquarius, Scorpio, Cancer
Virgo	Gemini, Aquarius, Leo, Libra	Capricorn, Libra, Gemini, Leo, Aquarius
Libra	Libra, Aquarius, Virgo, Scorpio	Libra, Pisces, Taurus, Aquarius
Scorpio	Leo, Sagittarius, Cancer, Taurus, Scorpio	Leo, Sagittarius, Cancer, Taurus, Scorpio, Pisces
Sagittarius	Pisces, Cancer, Scorpio	Pisces, Scorpio, Cancer
Capricorn	Aquarius, Leo, Cancer, Capricorn	Libra, Taurus, Aquarius, Leo, Capricorn
Aquarius	Aquarius, Libra, Leo	Aquarius, Leo, Capricorn
Pisces	Sagittarius, Scorpio, Leo	Sagittarius, Scorpio

You've just had a glimpse into Sun sign compatibility—but that's only the first step. Your Sun sign reveals how you interact with the world, manage interpersonal dynamics, and expect to be treated in your relationships. It also sheds light onto your love superpowers and blind spots—both in and out of the bedroom. Some signs are fueled by friction (Aries and Scorpio), while others lead with a gentler approach (Virgo and Libra). When feeling out a new relationship, some signs also look for stability (Cancer and Capricorn), while others are all about having fun (Leo and Gemini). And when the going gets tough, certain signs are more likely to work through issues (Taurus and Aquarius), while others are quick to pack up and leave (Sagittarius and Pisces). Ready to learn where you and your own love matches fit in? Let's begin!

Aries

(March 21–April 19)

Powerful and charismatic, Aries is the first sign of the zodiac—and when it comes to love and romance, Aries is fueled by fire. It is his natural element, after all! Also known for both his unpredictable temper and sweet tenderness, Aries is extremely multifaceted when it comes to love.

The Warrior

Sure, Aries is aggressive (appropriately, his astrological symbol is the hardheaded ram). But, even more importantly, Aries is a go-getter. The celestial ram is ruled by Mars, the planet that governs ambition and determination, so he thrives on challenges, competition, and invigoration. Simply put, Aries doesn't do demure. The confident and courageous ram is also a natural leader, so he isn't afraid to take charge and get things done. Whether it's romance or business, Aries always aims to come out on top. After all, this sign is *literally* number one in the zodiac. Aries's tactics can be a bit harsh, but this direct approach often works in his favor: the celestial ram usually gets his way.

Written in the Stars

Over the years, the symbol for Aries's governing planet, Mars—a sword and shield—has been adopted as the male symbol. Regardless of gender, Aries always exhibits an extraordinary vigor. With an incredible lust for life, he is one of the most enterprising signs of the zodiac.

Part of what makes Aries so successful is his natural magnetism and ability to command a room. He attracts partners with his innate enthusiasm and optimism, spicing up all of his relationships through his contagious *joie de vivre*.

Lessons in Love: How Do You Advise Aries?

Aries wants to do things his own way. Unless he *specifically* asks for advice, it's best to avoid telling this fiery lover what to do. Instead, try offering gentle, subtle suggestions. After all, you can guide a celestial ram to water, but you can't make him drink!

Aries is especially motivated to chase the unattainable, so he is attracted to anything shiny and new. Keep in mind that as a fire sign, Aries gets bored with those shiny objects easily, so in order to keep him happy, a relationship must remain exciting, passionate, and full of life. However, it should also be noted that although Aries is led by impulse, he is exceptionally honest. Though his fiery nature could suggest a wandering eye, he doesn't like getting in trouble—especially with the people he loves. Moreover, he sucks at keeping secrets, so if your Aries partner makes a mistake, he will be sure to let you know—either with his words or his *extremely* obvious attitude!

Independence is also *very* important for this fire sign—after all, he is the first sign of the zodiac and is very comfortable with being number one (and with not sharing the title). Even in a relationship, the celestial ram needs to spearhead solo initiatives. So, whether he is launching a business venture, playing lead guitar in a band, or corralling friends for an impromptu happy hour, Aries is always eager to get the proverbial (and sometimes literal!) party started. Just be sure you give him the space to do so.

The Quest for the Best: Aries Quirks

As an extremely ambitious sign, it is no surprise that Aries also strives for the "perfect" relationship. Aries may *claim* that the ideal partnership is argument-free, but in reality, this fire sign is most satisfied by an exciting dose of tension. The celestial ram wants to win, and playful competition challenges him to perform at his very best—always. Of course, Aries can't come in first place *all* the time, but to keep him engaged, be sure to acknowledge his victories. All fire signs (Aries, Leo, and Sagittarius) require an audience, but Aries is perhaps the most unabashed in exhibiting his need for validation. At times, this can seem boastful, but it is only because the assertive Aries ends every sentence with an exclamation mark instead of a question mark. For instance, he may declare he's "the best!" but in actuality, he's hoping that you can confirm that he *is* the best. You'll be forever charmed by your Aries partner if you swap the punctuation at the end of his statements. He is simply seeking your approval!

On occasion, Aries may also use his signature idealization to justify bad behavior. For instance, when a relationship hits a rough patch, Aries may rationalize flirting with someone else by claiming that his needs weren't being met in the partnership. This can be frustrating, but don't take it personally: Aries means no harm. In fact, since Aries is so straightforward, it's not hard to avoid a romantic meltdown. Simply maintain direct and honest communication, and this fire sign will maintain his loyalty. And if you're curious about Aries's idealized relationship fantasies, just ask! Aries loves talking about his hopes and dreams.

Written in the Stars

Don't be afraid to push back on Aries—especially if he is being pompous. So long as not *all* of your feedback is negative, this fire sign actually appreciates honesty!

The Aries Ego

Here's the deal: Aries has an ego—it's just part of his cosmic configuration. Sure, it may occasionally come off as arrogant, but the Aries ego isn't necessarily a bad thing. In fact, the entire zodiac kicks off *thanks* to Aries's confidence and panache: his energy is exactly what propels forward motion!

On a good day, Aries's vivacious spirit is invigorating and inspiring. On a bad day, however, he can be a lot to handle. Aries demands constant attention, which—if not well managed—can become draining. It's important for Aries's partners to learn how to say no...even if that means sitting through the occasional temper tantrum. Additionally, Aries is always testing the limits, so don't be surprised if your Aries partner occasionally says (or does) something super inappropriate. This is simply his way of gauging what is (and isn't) accessible. So, if your Aries mate rubs you the wrong way, be sure to let him know immediately. This fire sign respects personal boundaries, so once he understands the parameters of your unique relationship, he'll be sure to honor your needs.

Striking a Match: Attracting Aries

Whether you're rubbing stones together or striking a match, friction is a critical component of making fire. Once a flame is sparked, however, it's actually extremely sensitive: this tiny blaze needs to be in a supportive environment in order to sustain its glow. Likewise, Aries needs to be nurtured and supported at all times. Though he has a big presence, Aries is actually extremely delicate and requires lots of TLC in order to thrive. He depends on his partners to help maintain his vibrancy, so be sure to fan Aries's flame by offering genuine encouragement. If you're willing to serve the role of emotional cheerleader, your Aries mate will be forever grateful.

Aries is also turned on by ambition. Go-getters who match his vivacious spirit will attract his attention. Aries wants to be a part of a power couple that shines both privately and publicly. However, if Aries's partner's aspirations overpower his own vigor, don't be surprised if this fiery sign gets a bit envious from time to time (this will often be exhibited in the form of poutiness). When this occurs, don't fret: find the soonest opportunity to celebrate one of Aries's *many* achievements, and he'll be sure to radiate his gratitude.

Playing (the Right) Games

Usually, playing games with a romantic prospect isn't advisable. But when it comes to Aries, he enjoys a wee challenge. A natural competitor, this fire sign is all about flirtatious push and pull. Be aware, though, that this is *not* about manipulation: Aries is direct, so there's *nothing* he hates more than being tricked. You can tease and be playful, but at the end of the day, make sure you're always leading with your honest intentions.

Lessons in Love: Can a Fling with Aries Turn Into Something More?

Aries doesn't beat around the bush, so you can tell right away whether he intends to move forward with a relationship. If Aries only hits you up at two a.m. and refuses to stay the night, it's unlikely he is seeking something serious. If, however, he starts pursuing you *outside* of the bedroom, he is probably already planning your future together.

Comfort Comes First

The warrior that he is, Aries's ensembles tend toward athleisure. The fiery ram will attempt to make even the most exhausted pair of sneakers look stylish. But don't be surprised if Aries pushes that "just rolled out of bed" look a little *too* far. Aries values comfort, which can quickly escalate to, well, *schlub*. If your Aries mate is becoming lazy with his wardrobe, help guide him back on track. Since he likes anything new and exciting, recommend the latest pieces from a trendy fashion line—especially one that is a limited edition. He may put up a fight at first, but he'll appreciate the nudge (especially once the compliments start rolling in).

Despite his love of comfort, Aries does appreciate style. So, if you're looking for new ways to get his attention, don't be afraid to stand out. Aries is attracted to bold, dynamic fashion choices: bright colors, vibrant patterns, and fearless mismatching capture his warm heart. This fire sign loves playfulness, so if Aries sees you're having fun with your wardrobe, it will spark an instant attraction!

Let's Talk about Sex

When it comes to getting down, this fiery ram's fast-paced, high-intensity approach *definitely* delivers. Aries loves fast, fierce, and spontaneous hookups that leave both partners wondering, "What just happened?"—in a very good way. He jumps at the opportunity to get carnal. And there's no need for foreplay with this hot-blooded lover: he can rev up his engine in a matter of seconds.

Since Aries is no stranger to quickies in unusual places, he may also want to experiment with sex outside of the bedroom. Aries rules the head, so ask your Aries partner if he is into a bit of hair pulling or scalp massaging—it's very likely the answer will be a resounding yes. This lusty warrior should also try moves from behind: a sexy animalistic pose will be perfect for spontaneous trysts. But Aries has a soft side too. After extensive physical exertion, there's nothing he appreciates more than gentle caresses, especially on the head and neck.

Feeding the Flame: Maintaining a Relationship with Aries

Aries is fueled by passion, so when it comes to long-term relationships, it's critical that he finds new and exciting ways to maintain the flame. Committed Aries will love experimenting with fresh positions, role-play, and exciting new locations (in the words of The Beatles, "Why Don't We Do It in the Road?"). Sex is important to Aries, so when in doubt, physical touch will be sure to satiate this passionate fire sign.

Also remember this: everything is a conquest for the celestial ram, so he resents complacency. Aries always wants to feel like partnership is a choice, not an obligation. Accordingly, he will keep the spark alive by infusing your bond with adventure, drama, and, yes, an argument from time to time. Quarreling is actually a *good* thing for Aries: it keeps his fire going!

Making a Choice

If you've ever been involved with Aries for a long period of time, you'll eventually reach a crossroads: Is he in or out? Since Aries dives into relationships headfirst, this moment of introspection is *extremely* important for the fiery ram. He needs the freedom to consider the implications of his long-term commitment, so give him space to weigh his options and reach a conclusion. After some thoughtful rumination, your Aries partner will be sure to return to the relationship inspired, energized, and even more enthralled with your bond. If, however, Aries decides to exit the dynamic, don't be surprised if he comes crawling back later. Aries always wants what he can't have—even if he's the one who called it quits.

Sun Sign Love Matches

Aries falls in love quickly, but while one moment the celestial ram is head over heels, the next he is gone. Though this behavior makes total sense to Aries, the erraticism can lead to some *serious* heartbreak. So how does he handle relationships with different signs? In the following sections, you will find insights into Aries's top compatibility matches, as well as guidance on how he may operate in a relationship with a sign not included in his primary love matches.

Aries and Aries

Think rocket launchers, firecrackers, and lots of PDA. When teamed up, these two are truly a force to be reckoned with. Turn them against each other, though, and get ready for battle. Since an Aries-Aries match is a double dose of impatient restlessness, each will constantly demand security and stability from their partner. Thankfully, they understand each other, so if willing, they can meet in the middle. If each is delicate with the other's feelings and gives him plenty of space (without becoming too emotionally distant, of course), this can be a great long-term relationship filled with lots of fun, adventure, and passion.

Aries and Taurus

Taurus is notoriously stubborn, and when Aries feels challenged, he can also be extremely obstinate. When this happens, horns may clash in a *serious* way. However, there is an incredible sensuality in the Aries-Taurus relationship. Aries loves being wined and dined by the extravagant Taurus, and Taurus appreciates Aries's vivacious approach to life. To ensure a long-term relationship, both Aries and Taurus need to feel comfortable, nurtured, and protected. If both signs are game, this bond can be extremely romantic and supportive.

Aries and Gemini

Both Aries and Gemini are playful, spontaneous, and—perhaps most importantly—easily bored. Since they require a lot of stimulation, this pairing is excellent at holding each sign's interest. These two are always down for a good time, so they will enjoy taking weekend trips together, cohosting parties, and inspiring each other creatively. But since both Aries and Gemini are easily distracted, these signs need to work overtime to make sure the relationship isn't neglected. After all, partnership isn't all fun and games; it's also commitment, dedication, and lots of hard work.

Aries and Cancer

Cancer is governed by the moon: the celestial body linked to a person's emotional inner world. Because of this, Cancer is *extremely* sensitive and, since Aries is so outspoken, can be easily hurt by the ram's no-holds-barred approach to life. Conflict can arise when Aries feels as if his flame is constantly put out by Cancer's fragility. However, Aries and Cancer are both initiators, so when they work together, these two actually encourage each other to reach their highest potential. If both partners lead with love, an Aries-Cancer match can result in an extremely supportive, long-lasting bond.

When Stars Align

The zodiac is divided into three modalities: cardinal, fixed, and mutable. Cardinal signs propel action, fixed signs maintain systems, and mutable signs initiate change. Both cardinal signs, Aries and Cancer understand each other more than they may initially think.

Aries and Leo

Watch out for these two! When fire and fire come together, the blaze burns brightly. Both Aries and Leo are passionate, dynamic, and full of life, so when romantically bonded, they are unstoppable. Aries and Leo enjoy fanning each other's flames with big declarations of adoration and a lot of dramatic, over-the-top behavior. However, there can be trouble in paradise when Leo gets frustrated by Aries's childlike brutishness, and Aries becomes annoyed with Leo's theatrical snobbery. At the end of the day, however, the Aries-Leo match is cheerful and resilient. When positively motivated, Aries and Leo are each other's best advocates and—even more importantly—lifelong friends.

Aries and Virgo

Aries and Virgo make an unusual match. Virgo is meticulous, detail oriented, and extremely precise. Aries, on the other hand, cannot be bothered with the fine print: the celestial ram's only concern is coming in first place. While an Aries-Virgo pairing has serious vibes of *The Odd Couple,* these two can actually be quite kismet. Within this partnership, Virgo may learn to loosen up, while Aries may discover that buttoning up every now and then isn't actually *that* bad. If both Aries and Virgo lead with compassion, understanding, and a respect for each other's differences—and also embrace their partners as teachers—they can create a powerful, emotionally gratifying bond.

Aries and Libra

They say opposites attract—a theory no better tested than in an Aries-Libra couple. In the zodiac, Aries and Libra are direct opposites: Aries is the sign of *me*, whereas Libra is the sign of *we*; Aries is a warrior, whereas Libra is a peacemaker; Aries is a doer, whereas Libra is a thinker. However, when these two meet in harmony, they make an incredibly dynamic pair. Strong sexual attraction bonds Aries and Libra, and their varying perspectives offer a much-needed balance that supports each of their best qualities.

Aries and Scorpio

In traditional astrology, before Pluto was discovered in 1930, Mars (the planet of war) ruled both Aries and Scorpio. For this reason, these two signs share an incredible passion, albeit with different ways of manifesting their energy. Aries loves diving straight into combat, whereas Scorpio prefers to set up a scenario and observe it from afar. Aries might not get Scorpio's hands-off approach, while elusive Scorpio may feel "exposed" by Aries's straightforward nature. Despite their differences however, an Aries-Scorpio match is determined, ambitious, and *extremely* sexually charged. So, when it comes to the height of physical desire, look no further than these hot-blooded lovers.

Aries and Sagittarius

When it comes to a fiery Aries-Sagittarius bond, Aries sparks the match and then passes it to Sagittarius, who uses it to ignite a blazing wildfire. Sagittarius—the last fire sign of the zodiac—is an uncontained flame, an energy that dials up Aries's own intensity. Aries and Sagittarius know just how to rile each other up, and when on the same page, these two are truly unstoppable. They do, however, need to make sure that they continue to listen to each other's sensitive needs, offering mutual support on a deeper, more emotional level than just the purely fun-loving level they are more comfortable with. Otherwise, this massive flame may *definitely* get out of control, scorching the relationship and leading to tremendous heartbreak.

When Stars Align

When a sign (like Aries) links up with another sign (like Sagittarius) in its same element, they form a powerful trine shape. Triangles are one of the strongest forms in geometry, and, likewise, same-element couples (such as Aries-Sagittarius) are often truly dynamic.

Aries and Capricorn

At first, these two may appear to be a bit mismatched: Aries is motivated by an initial urge, while Capricorn—undoubtedly the hardest working sign of the zodiac—is driven by long-term focused success. Indeed, Capricorn climbs slowly to the top, while Aries head-butts his way into power. But, while these two have extremely different ways of interacting with the world, they actually perform extremely well as a couple. Enterprising Capricorn admires Aries's go-getter attitude, while fast-paced Aries appreciates Capricorn's incredible determination. The Aries-Capricorn match brings both of their unique gifts to the table, creating a union that is inspiring and fulfilling.

Aries and Aquarius

Aries, who is usually an extremely consistent, straight-shooting sign, actually changes his shape (albeit ever so slightly) when partnered with Aquarius. Aquarius is known for his aloof and detached sensibility: this air sign is such a progressive thinker that he can't be bothered with humdrum banalities. In this relationship, however, it is actually Aries who bends to accommodate Aquarius (very rare, indeed!). With Aquarius by his side, Aries will work hard to try to think outside of the box, understanding that getting caught up in day-to-day grievances doesn't yield long-term success. Appreciating Aries's efforts, Aquarius will also gradually become less jaded, enabling these two to meet in perfect harmony. Though there will certainly be an adjustment period, an Aries-Aquarius match has the potential to have a long-lasting future.

Aries and Pisces

An Aries-Pisces combination is extremely special. As the first (Aries) and last (Pisces) signs of the zodiac, these two form an incredibly powerful, karmic bond that is built on teaching and understanding. Fiery Aries is soothed by Pisces's healing energy, and gentle Pisces is electrified by Aries's blazing spirit. Although these two need to make sure they respect each other's *very* extreme differences (when angered, Aries's tendency is to blow up in anger, which terrifies emotional Pisces, causing her to swim away in defense), there's a special opportunity here for these signs to help each other understand the totality of the human experience. Together, Aries and Pisces are astrological bookends: between them, an entire life cycle exists, complete with joys, fears, and all of the magic that exists in between.

Love Planets: Venus and Mars

Your Sun sign helps you understand your essence (your wants, needs, quirks—what makes you, well, *you*), which is extremely important in exploring romantic compatibility. However, the Sun sign is just one component of your rich, complex astrological profile. The placement of the planets Venus and Mars within your birth chart (a snapshot of the sky at your exact moment of birth) also reveals critical information about your romantic sensibilities. In astrology, Venus is linked to love, beauty, and money. Simply put, you can look to Venus to understand the way you idealize partnership. By understanding Venus's function in your astrological profile, you can unlock a deeper understanding of how you approach romantic relationships. Mars, meanwhile, governs ambition, momentum, and sex. The placement of Mars in your birth chart reveals critical insights into how you "get down." And, let's be honest, whether a relationship lasts one night or an entire lifetime, sexual attraction is a major part of the equation.

Venus in Aries

Venus adores sensuality: tender, slow caresses, long-stemmed roses, cozy nights in front of the fire. Aries, on the other hand, likes *everything* fast and furious. So, when Venus occupies Aries, this romantic planet's personality shifts radically. Venus in Aries is assertive, direct, and action oriented. He tends to gravitate toward partners who exude incredible confidence. For Venus in Aries, love is a conquest—and he likes it that way. After all, the ultimate victory in life is falling in love.

Mars in Aries

Mars loves to be in Aries; in fact, Aries is governed by this action-oriented planet. Mars in Aries is impulsive, assertive, and not afraid to take charge in any situation. It's easy to spot him: he is the first to raise his hand in class, takes bold professional risks, and isn't afraid to slide into your phone messages at two a.m. Mars in Aries knows what he wants and—fueled by his passions—makes his intentions explicitly clear. When it comes to sex, he also desires lots of heat and passion. No need to play games with Mars in Aries, folks: it's *all* about getting down and dirty.

Chapter 2

Taurus

(April 20–May 20)

It's easy to fall in love with Taurus. After all, she is all about romance, sensuality, and indulgence. Governed by Venus (the planet of love), Taurus embraces the good life. In fact, she won't settle for anything less than what she knows she deserves—a trait that has earned her the (well-deserved) title of the zodiac's most stubborn sign (along with Aquarius).

The Luxuriant

Ruled by Venus, Taurus loves romance. From candlelit dinners to long-stemmed roses, this sign captures the spirit of courtship. Taurus adores wooing (and being wooed), so naturally she knows how to flirt. But despite Taurus's signature sensuality, she is hardly frivolous when it comes to love. In fact, she takes her relationship responsibilities extremely seriously. Once a commitment has been made, Taurus will work hard to preserve the bond. Unlike her astrological predecessor, Aries, she never falls in love for sport. Taurus wants a long-term partner and, often, a more traditional lifestyle within that bond. There's nothing that gets her more excited than that feeling of stability.

Dipping Into Indulgence

The need for stability also extends to her career and financial realms. In a perfect world, Taurus would spend all day bathing in a tub overflowing with essential oils, moisturizing with the finest beauty products, and enjoying the perks of room service on speed dial. However, despite this taste for indulgence, she knows the value of a dollar. As an earth sign, Taurus isn't afraid to roll up her sleeves. In fact, she is deeply connected to her output, feeling happiest after a long, hard day's work. After all, effort makes the rewards even sweeter. She also feels secure when she is steadily putting money away into a savings account. She is all about return on investment (the bull is also the symbol of Wall Street) and knows how to play the long game in her professional pursuits. This security is *paramount* for Taurus, and any threat to it will be sure to have her running for the hills.

The Stubborn Spirit: Taurus Quirks

Bathing in lavender oil not quite your thing? Sorry to say, but that *may* actually be a deal breaker for Taurus. Taurus is the sign of the bull, and much like the massive creature, this earth sign *does not* like to budge. If you don't share Taurus's interests—in either your taste or opinions—the celestial ox will take it *extremely* personally. While her consistency is admirable, Taurus must remember that life often exists within gray areas: things are not always so black-and-white. She must be a little flexible sometimes and accept that people can change their minds. In any relationship, each person needs to stay adaptable in order to take on whatever comes their way, so although it may be a difficult conversation, it's important to remind your Taurus mate that rigidity can be truly destructive.

Keeping Tradition Alive

Do you find vintage train sets charming? Your Taurus partner does! The celestial bull is extremely nostalgic, so she loves anything vintage or old-fashioned. In addition to appreciating charming memorabilia, Taurus also loves to honor traditions. Whether it be birthdays or holidays, she is committed to keeping these celebrations alive. Accordingly, one of the best ways to develop a long-lasting bond with Taurus is to actively work on creating your own shared memories. Propose a new ritual with your Taurus partner. Even something simple, like watching your favorite TV show together on Sunday evenings, will bring your earthy mate incredible joy and will be sure to make that occasion extra special.

Bottle of Red, Bottle of White: Attracting Taurus

Taurus is known to be a steadfast, grounded, and loyal partner. But before you can reap the benefits of Taurus's fidelity, you must first wine and dine this earth sign like there's no tomorrow (or, ahem, overdraft fees). Since Taurus is so closely connected to Venus, her seduction style is all about sensuality. So, if you're ready to romance her, get set for an all-inclusive trip through sights, sounds, and flavors. *Aah*, sensuality at its finest.

Written in the Stars

Chances are, your Taurus partner has already dropped some hints when it comes to great gift ideas for her. But when in doubt, go with luxury. An expensive bottle of wine, a necklace bedazzled with gemstones, or a high-quality pampering product such as a designer shaving kit will send Taurus an important message: not only do you care about craftsmanship, but you also aren't frugal!

Because Taurus is so connected to the material world, the celestial bull enjoys expressing affection through gift giving. To be clear, Taurus would never *dare* present you with thoughtless, airport gift shop tchotchkes. Instead—quite the opposite—Taurus will showcase her adoration with a present that captures your spirit. This, of course, isn't *totally* altruistic: Taurus expects something in return. She needs to know she's appreciated and that the relationship is reciprocal—after all, it takes two to tango! So each and every time Taurus expresses a like or dislike, she expects you to remember. Accordingly, pay close attention to your Taurus partner's feedback. Maybe even jot down a few notes. If she casually mentions her love for cheesecake, that means she will be waiting for you to pick up a slice from her favorite bakery!

In Bloom

Although Taurus is embedded in sensuality, it's very important that you don't come on too strong. In fact, this earthy creature will be *very* suspicious of a partner with a heavy-handed approach. Don't be afraid to take your time building trust. Taurus is in *absolutely* no rush, so embrace the opportunity to move slow and steady, letting the relationship unfold naturally.

Taurus season falls after the spring equinox, when—after a long winter—all life has begun to blossom, starting a new natural cycle. Similarly, it's important to remember that although it may take Taurus some time to fully open up, this earth sign is enchanted by the transformation process. For this Venusian partner, falling in love is an unbelievably magical experience—one that is *truly* well worth the wait.

Making It Official

Because Taurus appreciates security, this celestial bull tends to gravitate toward partners who share her views on finances, career, and family. Since these are *such* important considerations for her, it's easy to gauge her intentions from the very start: if Taurus is asking questions about your earning potential, career aspirations, or dream house by the third date, you can be sure that she is interested in moving forward—in a very serious way.

Written in the Stars

Be warned, there is nothing quite like a Taurus scorned. Loyalty means *everything* to this earthy creature, so if Taurus's partner is unfaithful, the breakup won't be fueled by stubbornness—it will be fueled by rage. And when a bull sees red, the only advice is get out of her way—fast.

Cosmic Sex Tips

Sex is a big deal for the Taurus lover. Accordingly, the actual act is not nearly as important as the buildup to it. Foreplay is the *ultimate* turn-on for the celestial bull and—like all things with this Venusian creature—should be a full sensory experience.

One evening, surprise your Taurus lover with some spontaneous romance, complete with champagne on ice, rose petals splayed across smooth linens, and soft, delicate candlelight. It may sound a bit trite to some, but don't forget this: Taurus loves tradition. These time-honored gestures of adoration will be well received and will be sure to set the mood for an extremely pleasurable night. *Meow.*

Peaches and Cream

Taurus is extremely epicurean, so for this sensual lover, foreplay always involves food. The way to Taurus's heart is through her stomach, after all, so the sexiest trysts will always include a tasty treat—peaches and cream, anyone?

Additionally, Taurus's erogenous zone is the neck, so kisses or playful bites in this area are sure to make the celestial bull go crazy. The missionary position (complete with plenty of eye contact) is also very sexy for the bull, so relish in the sultry nuances of this classic pose with your Taurus partner.

Tending the Earth: Maintaining a Relationship with Taurus

Although Taurus enjoys being with her partner, she also needs plenty of time alone to pamper and groom. Taurus takes her self-care rituals *extremely* seriously and—especially if her precious space is being threatened—can become quite possessive about her environment. Oh, and don't even *think* about touching Taurus's sacred objects. For the celestial bull, taking something without asking is a declaration of war.

Written in the Stars

It is important to remember that Taurus's penchant for possessions is *not* based on materialism. For her, objects simply symbolize security. The equation is simple: money is security, security is freedom, and freedom is happiness.

So how can you tell which objects Taurus cares about most deeply? The answer is simple: *all of them.* Because this celestial bull infuses every single possession with value, she cares about every single thing she owns. Although this can quickly degrade into slight hoarder tendencies, be advised of the following: under no condition should you throw out *anything* that belongs to Taurus. It's not worth the risk of her wrath. And with such plush taste, there is hardly anything worth tossing. Taurus loves anything that tantalizes the senses, so high-quality products are extremely important to her. She especially appreciates expensive, tailored clothes—and expects that you will too. As an earth sign, she pays close attention to details: fabrics, fits, draping, and patterns. And, because her eye for aesthetics isn't rooted in materialism, she focuses on quality over quantity. In other words, your Taurus partner won't care *how many* pairs of shoes you own...as long as the ones you *do have* are extra luxe.

Blowing Off Steam

To be blunt, Taurus tends to pick a lot of fights. But don't be fooled by her argumentative nature; it is *not* a reflection of her overall happiness in the relationship. In fact, if you find that your Taurus partner quarrels constantly, it means that she feels comfortable letting her guard down. You should actually take it as a good sign!

So why the constant bickering? It's simple: if Taurus doesn't release her minor frustrations in the moment, she will store up these grievances until one day she releases all of them in a dramatic, hotheaded explosion. Since it's best to avoid these bullfights, go ahead and let your Taurus partner grumble. It may be annoying at first, but in the end, this is actually the healthiest way for her to blow off some steam.

Money Matters

When it comes to a long-lasting partnership with Taurus, money matters. Of course, this doesn't mean that she is exclusively attracted to billionaires. In fact, the weight of one's wallet isn't all that important. What *really* makes a difference is how her mate manages, earns, and saves their income—and, perhaps even more importantly, whether they appreciate how hard Taurus works. Be sure to always acknowledge your Taurus partner's well-deserved success. Sure, she may spend more money on expensive dinners than most—but that's only because, after a long day's work, she *deserves* to indulge. Yes, the logic seems a bit convoluted, but once you start adjusting to this lifestyle, you, too, will realize that everything *does* taste sweeter once it's been justified—er, earned.

Sun Sign Love Matches

Taurus seeks stable, reliable partners—but that doesn't mean all relationships with Taurus are the same. Before investing precious time (and money!) into cultivating a relationship with this decadent bull, learn more about how Taurus builds the heat and strengthens her bond with each sign of the zodiac. There's a lot to uncover, so dive in.

Taurus and Aries

At first, Taurus may be a bit apprehensive about entering a relationship with impulsive Aries. Although she deeply appreciates the fiery ram's warrior-like energy, the celestial bull may proceed with caution: after all, she doesn't want to be the flavor of the week! Once Aries proves his steadfastness, however, these two can make an extremely dynamic duo, with Aries spearheading great ideas and logical Taurus offering sound advice. If both signs can avoid their tendency to say, "I told you so," they can teach each other invaluable lessons, forming a substantial long-term partnership that nurtures and inspires each sign.

Taurus and Taurus

You may never see more same-sign couples than the Taurus-Taurus combination. There's just something about the shared appreciation for fine dining, hot showers, and foot rubs that makes a Taurus-Taurus pairing unbelievably magnetic. When matched, these celestial bulls can spend all day snuggling, smooching, and snacking. But sometimes there can also be too much of a good thing: in this dynamic, each partner needs to make sure she is actively challenging the other to achieve her dreams. Otherwise, this duo may end up disappearing onto a cozy couch indefinitely.

Taurus and Gemini

At face value, the Taurus-Gemini partnership may seem difficult to reconcile. Fast-talking, quick-witted Gemini makes cautious Taurus uneasy, as Taurus has a difficult time understanding Gemini's motives. In an attempt to lock down a Gemini partner, Taurus may end up compromising her needs to accommodate his fast-paced lifestyle. Gemini, on the other hand, may grow increasingly impatient with Taurus's careful processing, making him more inclined to abandon ship. However, if this unlikely pair can compromise, a long-term partnership will be balanced and rewarding for both. Gemini will teach Taurus how to loosen up, whereas Taurus will inspire Gemini to slow down and smell the roses once in a while.

Taurus and Cancer

There are incredible parallels between Taurus and Cancer: both of these signs value security and stability, and they care deeply about cultivating a safe, domestic center. Within this cosmic pairing, Cancer will provide the emotional structure, while Taurus will delight in decorating their shared physical space. However, both Taurus and Cancer can also be extremely possessive. Without healthy communication, a Taurus-Cancer couple may turn on each other, becoming increasingly moody, jealous, and passive-aggressive. Although verbal expression is neither of their strong suits, this bond would surely blossom through open and honest dialogue.

Taurus and Leo

Taurus and Leo share a very strong mutual interest: both of these celestial beasts love to be fancy! Whether sipping fine wine, checking out a new restaurant, or shopping for designer clothes, Taurus and Leo see eye to eye on luxury. When the credit card bills start coming through, however, these two will quickly discover how their perspectives differ. Taurus values investment, whereas Leo celebrates flamboyance. So, while Taurus and Leo are both loyal and dedicated, their pride and stubbornness could lead to some serious clashes. In fact, a Taurus-Leo partnership may even feel like an arm-wrestling match. However, if these two hardheaded signs can learn to listen and compromise, they have the potential for a committed and successful future together.

Taurus and Virgo

Taurus and Virgo are both earth signs, and usually when like elements come together, they form an instant bond. Accordingly, the Taurus-Virgo attraction is built on logic: both of these signs value pragmatism. Interestingly, however, the Taurus partner is a bit extravagant compared to guarded Virgo. Taurus *definitely* knows how to indulge, whereas Virgo would rather play it safe. Taurus may have to work a little harder than usual to break through to cautious Virgo, so she may find that she is the one propelling the relationship forward. Ultimately, however, this match is strong: Virgo deeply respects Taurus's Venusian qualities and admires how she celebrates life's little luxuries, while Taurus appreciates Virgo's signature attention to detail. When these signs work together, the Taurus-Virgo pairing offers incredible potential.

Taurus and Libra

Both Taurus and Libra are governed by Venus, the planet that rules love, beauty, and money. Likewise, sensual Taurus and flirtatious Libra make an instantly romantic combination. Taurus's stubborn sensibility is balanced by Libra's calm diplomacy, while Libra's aestheticism is complemented by Taurus's domestic passions. These two align on many important things, though friction will certainly occur from time to time, especially when Taurus's possessive nature is compromised by Libra's insistent socializing. Libra wants to be well liked, which may drive Taurus bonkers—especially when the celestial bull is feeling insecure. At the end of the day, these conflicts are best resolved in the bedroom, which is where the Taurus-Libra couple *really* shines.

Taurus and Scorpio

There's often magnetism between opposite zodiac signs—but in the case of Taurus and Scorpio, the attraction is truly electric. Taurus season corresponds with spring and is associated with growth (this is actually the fundamental reason that Taurus is so obsessed with the physical world). Scorpio season, on the other hand, aligns with autumn and is linked to death and decay. Accordingly, the Taurus-Scorpio couple sits on the life-death axis in astrology, together forming an entire natural cycle. Because Taurus and Scorpio are both associated with transformation, they can share valuable lessons about change and regeneration. Of course, this doesn't mean that everything is perfect within this relationship. Neither Taurus nor Scorpio is great at compromising, which is essential for their respective needs to be met (Taurus demands material comforts, while Scorpio seeks emotional control). But, when these two work together, they can form a great match built on mutual respect. It is definitely worth the fight.

Taurus and Sagittarius

Taurus and Sagittarius drive each other bonkers, but, oddly enough, these two signs also have an undeniable attraction to each other. Sagittarius appreciates Taurus's decisive attitude, and although Sagittarius's nomadic lifestyle threatens Taurus's homeostasis, she is intrigued by his restless spirit. The tension between adventurer and homebody is best expressed in the bedroom: sex is fantastic between this unlikely pair, each teaching the other to try something different (Taurus advocates consistency, while Sagittarius inspires innovation). But, outside of the bedroom, these two must work hard to maintain a healthy, long-lasting partnership. Taurus will need to give Sagittarius plenty of room to roam, and Sagittarius will need to find a happy home within Taurus's domestic domain. If each can learn to accept the other's differences, the Taurus-Sagittarius pair exudes incredible chemistry.

Taurus and Capricorn

The Taurus-Capricorn couple is a match made in the stars. Taurus deeply respects Capricorn's steadfast ambition, and Capricorn is charmed by Taurus's elegance and domesticity. Taurus and Capricorn are both grounded, practical people, who truly understand each other. Of course, work is involved in every partnership, and in this case, the efforts need to be made by both sides. Taurus's inclination will be to cheer up stoic Capricorn—a futile effort for this saturnine sign. Similarly, as the more mature earth sign, Capricorn will try to "teach" Taurus how to be responsible, which the celestial bull will *naturally* resent. However, if these two can focus on their similarities as opposed to their differences, the Taurus-Capricorn bond is built to last.

Taurus and Aquarius

Taurus's traditional viewpoints seem outdated when compared to progressive Aquarius, whose creativity translates into rebellious and artistic eccentricities. While Taurus demands structure and comfort, Aquarius is fueled by more abstract and intellectual stimulation. Indeed, Taurus may find her horns locked with Aquarius. In fact, there may be no signs quite as stubborn as these two, so the Taurus-Aquarius pairing can feel dense. If Taurus and Aquarius pursue a relationship, they should focus on compromise, patience, and flexibility to ensure a healthy, forward-moving partnership. These two signs will also need to learn to communicate through shared interests. In doing so, they can cultivate a strong, flourishing relationship.

Taurus and Pisces

When dreamy Pisces links up with down-to-earth Taurus, they meet at the intersection of fantasy and reality. Pisces's creativity breathes new life into Taurus's practical outlook, and Taurus's rationality provides a great support system for Pisces to explore her eclectic interests. There is an incredible union between these two signs, although Pisces's flightiness may rub stable Taurus the wrong way at times. If conflict should emerge, Taurus must be very careful with confrontation: Pisces is highly sensitive, and if she feels attacked, she might swim away forever. Nevertheless, the Taurus-Pisces connection has incredible potential and, with just a bit of magic, could result in a long-term partnership.

Love Planets: Venus and Mars

While your Sun sign helps you understand your desires, needs, and unique tendencies (basically, your essence), it is just one component of your rich, complex astrological profile. The birth chart (a snapshot of the sky at your exact moment of birth) features a number of planets—each embedded with its own functions and purposes. Of these, Venus and Mars reveal critical information about your romantic sensibilities. In astrology, Venus is linked to love, beauty, and money. You can look to Venus to understand the way you idealize partnership and approach a specific relationship. On the other hand, Mars governs ambition, momentum, and sex. The placement of Mars in your chart will offer insight into how you "get down." And, let's be honest, whether a relationship lasts one night or a lifetime, sexual compatibility is a key part of the equation.

Venus in Taurus

Venus loves to be in Taurus—so much so, that Taurus is actually governed by Venus (meaning that this placement is its "domicile"). Accordingly, Venus in Taurus has an undeniably romantic essence. This lover exudes Venusian tendencies (namely a deep-seated appreciation for pleasure and luxury), while seeking romantic partners who offer a sense of stability and security. Venus in Taurus is happiest when coupled, as she is a very relationship-oriented person (motivated by the new beginnings created through partnership). Fundamentally, Venus in Taurus is about planting the seeds for a flourishing tomorrow.

Mars in Taurus

Mars is the planet of action, determination, and motivation. Taurus *can* be these things—but she really does, in a perfect world, prefer to relax. Likewise, Mars in Taurus will exhibit go-getter behavior in short bursts sandwiched between long periods of malaise. And when it comes to sex, she enjoys serious heavy petting. As an earth sign, Taurus is extremely tactile, so Mars in Taurus is all about physical affection. For this lover, sex is about making love. Slow, steady, and passionate, Mars in Taurus expresses her intense feelings through her deliberate motions.

Gemini

(May 21–June 20)

Ever been so busy that you wished you could just clone yourself? Well, that's Gemini in a nutshell. Symbolized by the twins, this air sign is interested in *so* many things that he simply needs a double. However, due to Gemini's intrinsic duality, he is often falsely represented as two-faced. In reality, the twin rarely has a hidden agenda: he just wants to have fun!

The Social Butterfly

As an air sign, Gemini can seamlessly move between friend groups, happy hours, and dance floors. Gemini is also governed by Mercury, the planet of communication, so this quick-witted celestial twin can *always* find a topic of shared interest. Gemini is an excellent storyteller, and his dynamic, extremely magnetic energy draws in romantic partners like moths to a flame. Hey, he can't help it! It's his signature je ne sais quoi. So, jealous lovers be warned, your Gemini mate will not be traveling alone. Instead, he will be sure to arrive with a horde of fans and followers. That dinner reservation for two will actually be for a party of twelve.

Written in the Stars

Both Gemini and Virgo are governed by Mercury, and the two sides of expression are reflected in this rulership. Gemini is all about output (sharing ideas with his community), while Virgo depends on input and processing (organizing and analyzing both her own and other people's "data").

As Gemini expresses his emotions externally, he loves to schmooze, often speaking with his hands (which also happens to be the body part associated with Gemini). This self-expression is paramount for the mercurial twin, and thus he needs all lines of communication to be open, clear, and ready to receive information—Gemini style. The truth is, he doesn't care *how* his thoughts are being transmitted (though he does prefer texting and tweeting to talking IRL, as it's faster and easier to share more thoughts with a large number of people digitally) because the *action* of sharing his ideas is even more important than what's being said. Expression helps Gemini feel connected to his own internal truths, enabling him to be the most authentic version of himself. Gemini also likes to experiment with different types of statements: "What would happen if I delivered this message? Would it be shocking? Exciting? Enlivening?" However, once the message has been delivered, he moves on to the next idea. There is a quick turnaround time for the celestial twin: he can get over something in a matter of seconds.

Written in the Stars

Since Gemini is so social, even in a serious partnership, it's important that he has the space to roam. Sometimes he will want to bring a plus one, but other times he will prefer to party alone. When the latter occurs, try not to take it personally!

Cosmic Juggling

There's nothing Gemini despises more than boredom, which is why the celestial twin is so busy all the time. He is constantly juggling his multiple passions, hobbies, careers, and social obligations—and that's just the way he likes it. This air sign might complain about being *so* overbooked, but when you really look at his day-to-day schedule, almost all of his activities are optional, proving that Gemini's double-booking is merely a by-product of his intrinsic duality.

The curious twin is also a terrific pioneer. He uses his "Energizer Bunny" momentum to spearhead innovative, creative projects, and—as a fearless thinker—he is always down to try something new. But after Gemini shares his progressive visions with the world (and let's be honest, Gemini will chat with anyone willing to listen!), it's best to let this dreamy twin get back to ideating: he is much better at cultivating thoughts than implementing ideas.

Written in the Stars

Gemini season begins on May 21, a day that usually ushers in the heat and electricity of summer. Appropriately, Gemini is excellent at guiding change and propelling transformation. Along with Virgo, Sagittarius, and Pisces, Gemini is a mutable sign.

Unlike his astrological neighbors (Taurus and Cancer), Gemini doesn't care much about stability. In fact, his love for intellectual stimulation is often tied to spontaneity and adventure. Ruled by Mercury, Gemini is satiated by cerebral adventures. Word games, puzzles, and trivia are his favorite activities—anything that activates his imagination and keeps him on his toes will hold his interest!

Duality, Not Duplicity: Gemini Quirks

Symbolized by the celestial twins, there are two sides to Gemini. But don't judge too fast: this doesn't mean that he is Jekyll and Hyde. The truth is that everyone, regardless of their zodiac sign, is multidimensional. Gemini just happens to wear these complexities on his sleeve. Duality is a central theme for this air sign, and he often thinks in pairs. But don't forget this: duality is not synonymous with duplicity. Although this sign may be stereotyped as having a reputation for two-timing, Gemini isn't any more likely to cheat than the other eleven signs. It is important to remember that no stars are inherently flawed. Everyone has the ability to manifest their own fate.

Written in the Stars

Sure, Gemini is playful, but that doesn't mean he doesn't get jealous from time to time! Try to make sure you don't push Gemini too far in your teasing: if he starts to feel threatened, he will be quick to retaliate.

And though Gemini loves to share his thoughts and ideas, he is not a particularly strong listener. As an air sign, he is easily distracted, so it's important to make sure that your Gemini partner is paying attention. If you happen to observe him drifting out of the dialogue, be sure to call him out: communication needs to be both ways!

Thinking in Pairs: Attracting Gemini

It's not easy holding Gemini's interest. In fact, because this air sign loves to bounce around, the celestial twin has practically seen it all before. Accordingly, the best way to steady his gaze (at least for a moment) is to keep him on his toes. Change things up as much as possible! Of course, don't compromise your values or needs, but as you get to know Gemini, have fun exploring your own multidimensionality.

The Gemini seduction technique corresponds with his general attitude: it's all about chatter! Since Gemini is the jack-of-all-trades of the zodiac, he will especially love talking about quirky hobbies and interests. Do you have a stamp collection? OMG, so does Gemini! Do you love skydiving? Gemini has always wanted to try! Because he is so curious, chatting with this air sign is like looking in the mirror: he has the amazing ability to reflect back whatever you say. That may seem a bit bizarre, but the truth is, it's just the nature of this sign. Gemini is a social chameleon.

Written in the Stars

Gemini loves to have a good time, often staying out late, schmoozing with strangers, and practicing new moves on the dance floor. When dating Gemini, be sure to ask specific questions (especially about his hobbies and interests: Gemini is always juggling *tons* of side projects). Since this air sign is so easily bored, a "traditional" style of courtship may actually be a huge turnoff.

If all of this sounds rather wild—well, it is. Dating Gemini is a truly exhilarating experience. But, be warned, Gemini requires *constant* stimulation, which sometimes makes it difficult to get to know the twin on a deeper, emotional level. Make sure you carve out time to sit and chat with your Gemini mate without any distractions. And don't be afraid to remind him that cozy evenings indoors are *not* time wasted. FOMO (fear of missing out) can only go so far when forming a romantic bond.

It Takes Two to Tango

Gemini *loves* sex. For the celestial twin, getting down is another form of communication. It should be no surprise, then, that Gemini has such strong sexual appetites. All it takes to arouse him are a few cleverly worded remarks. In fact, when it comes to talking dirty, Gemini wrote the book. He is extremely turned on by hyperdetailed accounts—even as the acts are underway. Excite your Gemini lover by explaining to him *exactly* what you enjoy in the bedroom. That way, he'll be feeling and intellectualizing simultaneously: a combination that—for this air sign—is truly orgasmic.

Written in the Stars

Gemini is unpredictable, so don't be afraid to also try new styles, positions, and techniques in the bedroom. He will appreciate your bold, adventurous spirit.

When you're not in the same environment as your Gemini lover (which, considering he is a Gemini, is probably quite frequently), experiment with digital intercourse via phone call, text, or webcam. Remember that Gemini is *highly* cerebral: even without physical touch, steamy dialogue will be extremely sexually gratifying.

Forgiving Mistakes: Maintaining a Relationship with Gemini

One of the most special Gemini attributes is how quickly (and seamlessly) the celestial twin can recover from even the most devastating blunders. Unlike many other signs, Gemini isn't governed by his ego. He loves having fun, so he doesn't let pride get in the way of a good time. Accordingly, when Gemini gets caught making a mistake, he won't be defensive. Instead, he will apologize immediately.

While this quality is appreciated, it's not totally selfless. Gemini expects you to accept his apology with the same speed. He moves too fast to care about missteps, and he expects his partners to press forward as well. Ultimately, this is something that a committed Gemini must be willing to negotiate. Although he may process things at the speed of light, his mates need the freedom—and encouragement—to have their own emotional experiences as well.

Finding Stability

So, is it even possible to find stability with Gemini? Absolutely. This consistency, however, exists *within* Gemini's freneticism. The truth is, Gemini is actually *happiest* when he is spread thin. As soon as his schedule becomes too comfortable, he finds a way to shake things up. It's not that Gemini fears normalcy; he just doesn't like to be bored. Gemini is also an incredible multitasker, and somehow he is able to satisfy all of his roles and responsibilities (he is the sign of the twins, after all). He knows how to cultivate systems that satisfy his ever-growing list of interests, but it's very difficult—in fact, nearly impossible—for him to focus all of his energy on any singular thing at a time.

Of course, this can be quite the challenge for Gemini's partners to navigate. Long-term relationships require lots of dedicated attention, which isn't easy for Gemini to offer! When coupled, the celestial twin needs to make sure he is prioritizing his bonds: after all, a partnership left on the back burner takes a lot longer to cook.

Written in the Stars

Sometimes it's hard for Gemini to think past his own immediate realities—but that doesn't mean he doesn't want to try. At the end of the day, Gemini wants to link up with someone who will constantly challenge him to expand his horizons.

Sun Sign Love Matches

It's no surprise that Gemini doesn't have a particular type. Since this air sign is down to try anything at least once (but more often twice), he enjoys exploring different aspects of his personality through his romantic relationships. In short, Gemini is extremely adaptable—but how does he match with each sign of the zodiac? Read on to find out!

Gemini and Aries

These two like to gossip, play, and get into trouble together. In fact, the Gemini-Aries bond is strong within all types of dynamics: friendship, romance, and those that exist solely in the bedroom. Aries and Gemini both enjoy mischief, and they have an incredible appreciation for each other's signature impulsivity. With their inside jokes, secret code words, and *lots* of laughter, Gemini and Aries bring out the best in each other. The danger, however, is that neither Gemini nor Aries is particularly good at calling it a night. Within the Gemini-Aries partnership, it's important that *someone* assumes the responsible role. Otherwise, it may be difficult for these fun-loving mates to cultivate a healthy, emotionally stable relationship.

When Stars Align

When Gemini and Aries get together, expect mischief and mayhem. These two have an "us against the world" mentality, so they're always looking for new ways to stir the pot—even if that means challenging the infrastructure of their relationship through spontaneous disagreements.

Gemini and Taurus

The Gemini-Taurus bond isn't always easy, but if both partners are invested, it can be incredibly worthwhile. Strong-willed Taurus enters the relationship with a heavy hand, unafraid to set precedent, establish boundaries, and define expectations. Gemini has a very different way of seeing the world, so the celestial twin doesn't quite understand Taurus's insatiable need for security. However, if they can meet in the middle—at the halfway point between permanence and transience—they can teach each other invaluable lessons. If both Taurus and Gemini are willing to make radical changes to meet the other's needs, this dynamic has the potential to challenge each sign in extremely meaningful ways.

Gemini and Gemini

What happens when two sets of twins come together? It's a party! When Gemini enters a game of doubles, it's hard for any spectator to keep their eye on the ball. Similarly, while these vivacious signs understand each other deeply, this pairing can lack perspective. In order for a Gemini-Gemini bond to succeed long term, each person needs to make sure he is listening and responding—not just talking *at* the other. Both sets of twins will also have lots of exciting ideas, but unless one partner is willing to step up and put the wheels in motion, they are at risk to blow lots of hot air. Needless to say, when it comes to expressing their creativity (especially songwriting), Gemini-Gemini will be sure to create some extremely cutting-edge works of art—and that's something you *can* take to the bank.

Gemini and Cancer

Cancer, Gemini's zodiac neighbor to the right, has a very distinctive approach to life. Sensitive and intuitive, Cancer requires lots of love, commitment, and validation in order to feel safe and supported. Initially, it may seem like spontaneous Gemini could *never* be able to offer that type of structure—but Gemini is malleable. If Cancer communicates her needs (in a direct, nonpassive-aggressive way), Gemini will work with her to honor her requests. Cancer's deep emotions and serious sensibility are also challenged by Gemini's detached coolness. However, so long as Gemini takes off the mask and is willing to get real with Cancer, this can be a match worth maintaining. Ultimately, though this bond does require some investment, these signs can build a warm, compassionate, and—most importantly—fun relationship.

Gemini and Leo

Individually, both Gemini and Leo are the life of the party. When together, however, they form a power couple to be seen—and heard. Leo loves to be in the center of the action, and, likewise, there's nothing Gemini enjoys more than finding fun. However, while these two social butterflies are happy to cruise between backyard barbecues, gallery openings, and networking functions together, they may quickly discover that their core motivations are a bit different. Leo loves to show off in front of an audience but, at the end of the day, looks for partnership that is honest and dependable. Gemini, on the other hand, doesn't care about impressing people. In fact, Gemini is interested—almost exclusively—in feeding his insatiable curiosities. Where Leo wants to establish trust and loyalty, Gemini is coupling up to have fun. Accordingly, Leo may perceive Gemini as detached, whereas Gemini may get frustrated with Leo's neediness. Through communication, however, these two can learn to work together, building a sustainable partnership that's based on exploration and adventure.

Gemini and Virgo

Both Gemini and Virgo are governed by Mercury—the planet of communication. Due to this, they share a deep understanding and an appreciation for expression. However, despite this mutual mercurial influence, these two signs have extremely different ways of transmitting information. Gemini is all output, whereas Virgo is predominantly input. Gemini is witty and quick with his thoughts, whereas Virgo, the astute observer and processor, prefers to express ideas only after her thoughts have been properly organized. Accordingly, a Gemini-Virgo bond requires that both signs work hard to make sure that they're sharing *and* listening to each other equally. Otherwise, it's very likely that Gemini will end up dominating the conversation, while Virgo builds quiet resentment toward her excessively loquacious companion. Flirty, social Gemini can also make Virgo nervous or jealous; however, when each sign is able to let their guard down and have some fun, this relationship has potential.

Gemini and Libra

There's an instant connection when two like-minded air signs come together. Simply put, Gemini and Libra align in perfect harmony. These two will always keep each other engaged with fun conversations, interesting stories, and lots of fabulous parties. Tension may arise however when Libra—in all of his aesthetic glory—gets frustrated by Gemini's nondiscriminatory banter. The truth is, Gemini will talk to *anyone* about *anything*. Libra, on the other hand, is a bit more selective about *whom* he engages in conversation—an attribute that Gemini may find a bit pretentious. However, if each sign is able to find respect for the other's approach, the Gemini-Libra pairing has the potential to last for a very long time.

When Stars Align

In response to Libra's more "sophisticated" nature (and the pretentiousness that can be perceived in it), Gemini may *intentionally* adopt more immature behavior, just to challenge his Libra partner. Gemini should watch out for this urge and try to keep it at bay!

Gemini and Scorpio

Neither Gemini nor Scorpio is easily thrown off-balance. Gemini is too distracted by life's many excitements to get too caught up in a singular drama, while Scorpio would never *dare* let down her guard unless she knew it was the real deal. Interestingly enough, however, Gemini and Scorpio are drawn to each other in an incredibly powerful, magnetic way. Gemini is fascinated by Scorpio's mystique, and Scorpio becomes obsessed with trying to win Gemini's affection (after all, getting this celestial twin to commit would be the *ultimate* victory). At first, the Gemini-Scorpio bond is driven by curiosity, but once the couple is established, there are a few big hurdles these two must face. Witty, talkative Gemini needs freedom, while powerhouse Scorpio demands unyielding loyalty from her mates. And while Gemini is flexible, Scorpio stews in her feelings, so it's important that both partners practice reading the other's nuances. The Gemini-Scorpio match isn't always easy, but incredible chemistry (especially sexually) may make this pairing worthwhile.

Gemini and Sagittarius

Gemini and Sagittarius are extremely compatible. For these two, opposites really do attract—in fact, the Gemini-

Sagittarius pair is one of the most dynamic couples in the entire zodiac. These signs are natural wanderers and, when linked, form an incredibly artistic, adventurous, and fun-loving power couple. They have similar life outlooks, and approach the world with a shared sense of enthusiasm, curiosity, and optimism. And, since both Gemini and Sagittarius are natural storytellers, the mental stimulation between these two signs will be sure to have neurons firing off at rapid speed. While neither may be the *most* sentimental sign, both truly appreciate personal space and boundaries. Basically, this is a pretty effortless pairing—so much so, in fact, that the Gemini-Sagittarius couple needs to make sure they don't take the bond for granted. Every relationship requires hard work, trust, and commitment, so both Gemini and Sagittarius need to ensure that they're not taking *too* many liberties. Otherwise, a great thing may go to waste.

Gemini and Capricorn

Capricorn is dumbfounded by Gemini. The most hard-working sign of the zodiac, she truly does not understand how someone *so* erratic can get anything accomplished at all. As Capricorn is scratching her head over this, Gemini—like a true magician—showcases the many ways he achieves success, leaving Capricorn in awe...and totally smitten. The Gemini-Capricorn bond isn't necessarily easy (Gemini sometimes feels judged by Capricorn, the stoic workaholic of the zodiac, while Capricorn feels threatened by Gemini's darting attention), but through communication, these two can gradually learn how to better understand each other.

To build a long-term, healthy relationship, Capricorn must accept that Gemini changes his mind *extremely* frequently. Likewise, Gemini must learn how to share his thought process with Capricorn, so his earthy mate can understand the rationale behind his excessive pivots. Ultimately, the Gemini-Capricorn dynamic can work, but it will definitely require dedication on both sides.

When Stars Align

It's not that Capricorn doesn't want to have fun—it's just that she feels quite strongly about maintaining a healthy work-life balance. Mercurial Gemini likes to test Capricorn's limits, but interestingly, Capricorn is happy to accept the challenge. The sea goat can be quite mischievous, herself! During a playful night, don't be surprised if Capricorn actually goes home later than usual—even if she has an early meeting the following day!

Gemini and Aquarius

Gemini is a wordsmith, and like-minded Aquarius is extremely attracted to his clever and vivacious intellectualism. Gemini, meanwhile, is inspired by Aquarius's unflappable attitude and deeply humanitarian sensibilities. Gemini and Aquarius truly get each other and intrinsically know how to sharpen each other's wit with great conversation. However, Aquarius is known for his radical perspectives and revolutionary ideas, which, though admirable, can also be a bit jarring to Gemini at times, who usually prefers schmoozing to rebelling. Despite a small learning curve, however, it's easy for these two to learn how to work together. A Gemini-Aquarius pairing can surely blossom into a long-term, serious romance.

Gemini and Pisces

There is a strange commonality between Gemini and Pisces: both have a complex dimensionality. Because Gemini is symbolized by the twins, this air sign wears his duality on his sleeve. On the other hand, Pisces's multiple faces are less discernable to the naked eye. The Pisces glyph symbolizes two fish—attached by a horizontal string—moving in opposite directions, representing her link to both the ethereal and terrestrial realms. Because both of these signs have two sides, they understand each other's need for space, freedom, and exploration. However, neither Gemini nor Pisces is particularly great at creating boundaries, so a Gemini-Pisces couple needs to work extra hard to establish the terms of their dynamic. On a bad day, hypersensitive Pisces may be suspicious of the intentions behind Gemini's clever finesse. Meanwhile, gregarious Gemini is likely to think of emotional Pisces as being overly dramatic. For a successful partnership, this pair requires honest and game-free communication.

When Stars Align

Gemini and Pisces both love music: Gemini is an incredible lyricist, while Pisces enjoys the sounds, harmonies, and abstract emotional expression it offers. These two would make an amazing musical duo! If romance doesn't work out, perhaps they could try starting a band together.

Love Planets: Venus and Mars

Your Sun sign helps you understand your desires and needs (essentially what makes you *you*), which is extremely important in exploring romantic compatibility. However, this sign is just one component of your rich, complex astrological profile. The birth chart (a snapshot of the sky at your exact moment of birth) also features a number of planets—each with its own function and purpose. Of these, Venus and Mars reveal critical information about your romantic sensibilities. In astrology, Venus is linked to love, beauty, and money. By understanding Venus's function in your astrological profile, you can unlock a deeper understanding of how you approach relationships. Mars governs ambition, momentum, and sex. When exploring romantic compatibility, it's important to look into the role of Mars within an astrological profile, as this placement reveals insight into how you like to "get down." And, let's be honest, whether a relationship lasts one night or an entire lifetime, sexual attraction is a major part of the equation.

Venus in Gemini

Venus in Gemini falls in love quickly—but that's only because, for this dynamic lover, communication is the fastest route to his heart. Venus in Gemini is attracted to partners who are vivacious, dynamic, and—perhaps most importantly—incredibly intelligent. He is also extremely flirtatious, but that's only because he exudes his sensuality through language. And although he may spend hours chatting with an intriguing stranger at a bar, he is not necessarily inclined to go home with them: the intellectual stimulation is enough to satisfy him.

Mars in Gemini

Mars in Gemini pursues everything in multiples. This busybody is constantly working on *at least* two things at once: in careers, hobbies, and—yes—sometimes even relationships. Even if Mars in Gemini isn't advocating for a more open dynamic, it's very likely that he will have quite a few serious relationships over the course of his lifetime. And when it comes to sex, this impulsive lover gets turned on by whatever is shiny and new. Lovemaking should always be an adventure, so his lovers shouldn't be afraid to switch things up often!

Chapter 4

Cancer

(June 21–July 22)

Cancer is a water sign represented by the celestial crab, who seamlessly crawls between the sea and shore, an ability also reflected in her capacity to fuse both the emotional and physical realms. Further, Cancer's intuition (pulled from the emotional realm) manifests in tangible ways. For instance, she can effortlessly pick up on the energies of people and spaces, making her a truly compelling partner.

The Chariot

In tarot, Cancer is traditionally symbolized by the Chariot card, which depicts a brave warrior shielded in an armored chariot. Likewise, Cancer is an expert at protecting her soft interior with a hard outer shell. She understands that she is extremely sensitive, so she won't feel comfortable opening up to a partner until she can *guarantee* that person is both interested and available.

> **Written in the Stars**
>
> Did you know that pearls are associated with Cancer? These luxurious, glistening objects are produced within the soft tissue of a hard-shelled mollusk. This gemstone is the perfect metaphor for this tough-exterior water sign!

Because trust and loyalty are critical for this delicate sign, she may come off at first as cold or distant. With time, however, Cancer reveals her gentle spirit, genuine compassion, and psychic skills—just don't be surprised if it takes a while. If you're fortunate enough to earn her confidence, you'll quickly discover that despite her initial reserve with people, she loves cohabitating. For this lunar lover, partnership is *truly* the greatest gift.

> **Written in the Stars**
>
> The crab mythology surrounding Cancer is believed to have originated in ancient Babylon. In ancient Egypt, though, twin turtles were actually associated with this sign's celestial constellation.

Cancer rewards these relationships through her steadfast loyalty, commitment, and emotional support.

The Mother Moon

Each day, your activities are led by the sun. At night, the moon emerges and reflects the experiences of your past day. Likewise, the moon symbolizes your emotional inner world, revealing how you really feel about situations. The moon oversees these internal experiences, helping you understand what makes you feel safe and protected. The moon is also ever-changing, just as your internal experiences constantly shift. This deep connection to the emotional experience is what ties the moon to the essence of the mother.

Cancer is governed by the moon. And just as the moon has a long historical connection with female energy and motherhood (in fact, the moon's cycle is also tied to both menses and pregnancy), Cancer is also linked to this maternal spirit (of course, this energy isn't specific to a gender—anyone can carry it). Indeed, Cancer represents the mother. Within astrology, the concept of the mother reveals both how you were raised and how you nurture others. Perhaps most importantly, this maternal identity also helps you understand how you take care of yourself.

Fittingly, Cancer tends to be quite domestic. Consider how the celestial crab carries its home on its back: it's very important for Cancer to cultivate a safe, cozy environment. To Cancer, her home serves as a personal sanctuary; it is a space where she can exhibit her full and complete self. And, since Cancer doesn't often emerge from her shell, she ends up spending lots of time in her home realm.

With her domestic flare, the crustacean also makes an excellent host. Don't be surprised if your Cancer partner enjoys entertaining with comfort food and free-flowing libations. In fact, in medical astrology, Cancer rules the stomach, so there's nothing the crab loves more than home cooking. But this is not just about cultivating her environment: Cancer also cares deeply about her friends and family members. She loves to adopt caregiver roles that allow her to build emotional bonds with her closest companions. But be aware of this: when Cancer invests in someone emotionally, she risks blurring the line between attentive nurturing and controlling behavior. Not vibing with Cancer's caregiving style? That may be an issue for her.

Bad Behavior: Cancer Quirks

Just as the moon's appearance is constantly transforming, Cancer also has a fickle nature and a tendency toward crabbiness. In fact, Cancer is definitely the moodiest sign of the zodiac. Although her partners will learn to appreciate her emotional wax and wanes, Cancer must also manage her own sensitivities. After all, her defensive habits definitely have an antagonistic side: when she feels threatened, this crab won't hesitate to use her sharp claws to pinch. *Ouch!* When coupled with a partner, Cancer must remember that misunderstandings are to be expected; the occasional disagreement does not make her mate the enemy.

Lessons in Love: What Do You Do When Cancer Gets Crabby?

Usually, Cancer doesn't just get moody for no reason: *something* triggered the shift in her energy. If you can identify the cause (perhaps it was a simple miscommunication), don't be afraid to address it head-on. If you're not sure what caused the emotional shift, however, start looking for clues. The faster you tackle the issue, the quicker your Cancer partner will bounce back.

In addition, Cancer must actively work on staying present in her relationships. As an emotional and introspective sign, it's easy for her to retreat into herself more often than not. If she doesn't stay present in a relationship, the next time she emerges from her shell, her partner may no longer be available.

Crab Claws

Cancer is a great listener. Like the other water signs (Scorpio and Pisces), once she steps outside of her shell, she is an emotional sponge. Your Cancer partner will absorb your emotions, which sometimes can feel supportive, but at other times feels stifling. You're sick? So is Cancer! Tough day at work? Cancer hates her boss too! It's not always easy to tell whether Cancer is empathizing or mimicking, but since she is so connected to her partner, there's ultimately no difference between the two. If Cancer's emotional backboard *is* cramping your style, it may be best to let it go. This sensitive sign is easily threatened by even the most subtle criticism.

And although the celestial crab avoids direct conflict by walking at an angle, she can also use her claws.

Unfortunately, this distinctive passive-aggressive behavior is to be expected: it's impossible to date Cancer without experiencing her signature pinch at least once. As a result of Cancer's sensitivity, it's not easy to discuss issues with her, but eventually you'll learn which words to say and—perhaps more importantly—which to avoid. Be aware of what rubs your Cancer mate the wrong way, and over time it will become easier to have difficult conversations.

Your Crab Companion: Attracting Cancer

So, you're ready to build a lasting bond with the celestial crab? You'll definitely need to play by her rules, so it's important to know how this magical creature operates at her best—and her worst. Ultimately, the most important thing to remember is that Cancer is *never* as cold as her facade. Indeed, the most difficult aspect of dating Cancer is breaking through her tough, unyielding exterior. For this reason, patience is key when courting Cancer. Maintain a slow and steady pace, and she will eventually build the trust needed to reveal her true self.

Written in the Stars

Cancer is an extremely creative sign—but she doesn't always feel comfortable showcasing her gifts. As you get to know your celestial crab, ask about her art: Does she draw? Paint? Make craft projects? If you express interest, she'll be delighted to share her hidden talents.

Of course, this can be an intimidating process: the smallest mistake can put Cancer on the defense, so two steps forward are often followed by one step back. But don't get discouraged! It's nothing personal—it's just the anatomy of a crab.

Crustacean Community

The concepts of home and family are very important to Cancer, and her familial bonds greatly impact her long-term partnerships. In fact, when Cancer has good childhood memories, her relationships with her parents or siblings may inspire the models she sets for all of her future relationships. However, if she felt unseen or unsupported in her youth, she will have a more complex relationship with the concept of partnership. She may try to create the antithesis of her upbringing by doing *exactly* what was unwelcome in her family home, or she may reject the notion of traditional partnership altogether. No matter what, Cancer will have *strong* opinions (and even stronger feelings) about how she was raised. When you reach a point in your relationship with Cancer to discuss her childhood, this dialogue will be incredibly illuminating.

Sex on the Beach

Though Cancer *can* have casual sex, this sweet water sign prefers relations that involve emotional intimacy. Remember, Cancer needs to be completely comfortable before emerging from her shell—and this Cancerian truth is *especially* important when it comes to sex and her sexuality.

For the crab, trust is fueled by physical closeness. You can begin to cultivate a sexual relationship with Cancer by slowly (being mindful of her pace) integrating cuddling, spooning, and hand-holding into your relationship. This will allow Cancer to become more comfortable with fusing emotional and physical expression, ensuring she feels safe and protected before any lovemaking begins.

Lunar Love

Once the shell has been broken down, however, Cancer can *finally* let her freak flag fly—in a major way. Since Cancer is governed by the moon, this celestial crab's libido is guided by the lunar cycle. Start observing how the moon's phases influence your Cancer lover's sexuality: How does she behave sexually during the new moon, when there's no light in the night sky? Does it differ from her proclivities during a full moon, when there's total illumination at night? Explore these dynamics.

Sideways Sensuality

The crab moves from side to side, meaning any lateral motion is going to be particularly stimulating for Cancer. Experiment with sultry wraparound positions that enable both lovers to make romantic eye contact. How can your movement link to your breath? Just as the moon governs the ocean's tides, Cancer loves to feel the rhythm of her partner's breathing—this is a *huge* turn-on for the celestial crab. Cancer is extremely sensual, so don't be afraid to get hot and steamy with your crustacean love.

Lessons in Love: Where Should You Vacation with Cancer?
Much like her symbolic shellfish, Cancer feels most comfortable close to the ocean, either splashing around in the waves or relaxing by the shore. Plan a beach trip with your Cancer babe—nothing makes her happier than being by the water!

Burying Secrets: Maintaining a Relationship with Cancer

Although Cancer is patient and tends to be extremely loyal, because she needs to feel protected, supported, and understood by her partner, she may seek intimacy elsewhere if she feels these needs aren't being met. And it can be difficult for one person to always satisfy Cancer fully. For instance, during a disagreement she may feel betrayed, sending her running off to a "safer" connection. Cancer can definitely be sneaky, so any secret relationship will be planned and plotted. A crab that strays will do *whatever* is necessary to take her dirty deeds to the grave: she'll take extra precautions to make sure a tryst goes undiscovered by burying any evidence deep in the sand.

In fact, even the most faithful crustacean will have *some* secrets...but that doesn't necessarily mean they are bad or harmful secrets! Everyone deserves to keep certain things private, even from their partner. Plus, a little mystery will keep the sparks flying. Cancer is also known to be a great listener, so this celestial crab will often look after a friend's "dirty laundry." At the end of the day, Cancer is a complex, sometimes enigmatic, puzzle, so don't worry if your crab partner lived a "double life" before you came into the picture: she is multidimensional, but that doesn't mean she is duplicitous.

Broken Shells

Because it's not easy for Cancer to enter a serious, committed relationship, when she finally feels safe in a partnership, she will not want it to end. In fact, Cancer tends to stay in relationships even after the sparks have died and things have run their course. Simply, Cancer is a romantic at heart: she will always fight to maintain a partnership.

But, of course, not all bonds are meant to last forever. So, in order for Cancer to release a partner from her claws, she will need to vilify them. This water sign doesn't intend to be bitter...but when she feels heartbroken, she is *all* about boundaries. These practices (such as blocking and unfollowing an ex on social media) allow her to shield herself from pain during a breakup. So if your relationship with Cancer comes to a close, expect to receive a detailed list of rules and regulations. It's not easy for Cancer to retreat back into her domestic space alone, so she will also value the support of her friends and family during this difficult time.

Sun Sign Love Matches

Cancer can be idealistic; this water sign is definitely seeking her version of a "white picket fence" romance. However, the crab will interact differently with each zodiac sign: all relationships are different! Read on to learn about the love compatibility this cosmic crustacean has with each Sun sign and how she can better make those more unlikely matches thrive.

Cancer and Aries

Aries's stop-at-nothing, go-getter attitude is a stark contrast to Cancer's deep sensitivity. As a result, Aries may feel smothered by Cancer's neediness, and Cancer may feel neglected by Aries's self-interested nature. Cancer also struggles with direct confrontation, and like her astrological symbol the crab, she prefers to sidestep difficult situations rather than approach conflict head-on (which is Aries's MO). Outspoken Aries isn't particularly fond of these passive-aggressive tendencies, so the Cancer-Aries match can sometimes prove to be challenging. When paired with Aries, Cancer should practice a more straightforward approach to conflict resolution. Aries will appreciate her honesty, and this open dialogue will allow these signs to create a truly unbreakable union. If they can learn to compromise, they may expect a substantial long-term partnership built on love, trust, and support.

Cancer and Taurus

These two are both romantic, and they know how to give each other the emotional support they crave. Though they tend to be possessive with each other, they each also understand the other's need for security and dependability. Taurus provides sensitive Cancer with commitment and loyalty, and Cancer's smooth seduction style appeals to Taurus's classy sensibilities.

Friction arises only when these two begin nitpicking each other: if Cancer is constantly snapping her claws, Taurus will begin to bottle up her resentment—which would eventually explode in a gigantic bullfight. Fortunately, they can avoid tension by maintaining honest communication and finding appreciation for each other's magical gifts.

Cancer and Gemini

Sensitive, watery Cancer requires a lot of TLC from her partner in order to feel both secure and loved. At first, you may wonder how spontaneous Gemini could ever fit the bill, and true, he does enjoy a lot of space and freedom to explore his many interests. However, as a mutable air sign, he is also very malleable. If Cancer can directly communicate her needs, Gemini will work to honor them. Gemini can also be quite cool and detached, while Cancer is quite the tidal wave of emotions, but as long as Gemini is willing to get deep with Cancer, this can be a caring and quite fun bond.

Cancer and Cancer

When two celestial crabs unite, it is quite the romantic fairytale. Sensitive, intuitive Cancers each know how to provide the emotional support that the other craves. Both homebodies, they will also enjoy spending their time together cuddled up on the couch, or creating a cozy atmosphere in their shared living space. Problems can arise, however, when they get too comfortable to nurture individual interests and ambitions outside of the home. If these watery lovers can remember to encourage each other in their separate hobbies and talents, and open their hard outer shells up to completely trust each other, this can be a long-lasting relationship.

Cancer and Leo

While this is not *necessarily* an easy match, it doesn't mean that a Cancer-Leo bond is impossible. Oddly enough, the crab and lion actually have a lot in common. In their own ways, both Cancer and Leo demand love, recognition, and validation. While performative Leo seeks compliments and loyalty, sensitive Cancer wants to be needed and understood. The formula for conflict between these signs is fairly straightforward: theatrical Leo searches for applause from his extended community; domestic Cancer then feels unloved and becomes moody, which leads Leo to take Cancer's grumpiness personally; and—lo and behold—they begin to argue. If both Cancer and Leo can understand and manage their own blind spots, however, it's not hard to avoid this kind of ego-based conflict. For the Cancer-Leo match, open dialogue, constant reassurance, and lots of snuggling will help strengthen this romantic bond.

When Stars Align

If Cancer can learn to trust Leo, these two will bring out the best in each other. Leo will help Cancer explore bravery, while Cancer will be sure to tame the proud lion.

Cancer and Virgo

Although there are some stark differences between Cancer and Virgo (Cancer is fueled by emotions, whereas Virgo is driven by logic), these two make a powerful match—it may just take some cajoling. Cancer doesn't like coming out of her shell, and similarly, Virgo is reluctant to take the lead with vulnerability. As Cancer and Virgo get to know each other, it can feel like two steps forward equals one step back. However, once trust is established, the Cancer-Virgo pairing is truly profound. Patient Virgo and sensitive Cancer can truly feel secure with each other, and although both signs are worriers, they calm each other's nerves through commitment and dependability. Although neither partner enjoys talking about her feelings at first, if both are equally invested, they can find safety in their mutual respect and admiration for the other.

Cancer and Libra

In the beginning of a courtship, Cancer's withdrawn attitude confuses outgoing Libra, who works tirelessly to try to impress the elusive crab. On the flip side, Libra's dashing communication skills and highly flirtatious behavior make Cancer skeptical of his intentions. Ironically, both Cancer and Libra worry that the other sign is leading them on, so it may be difficult to break through the early stages of dating. However, once Cancer accepts Libra's essence as diplomatic, and Libra understands Cancer's delicate spirit, these two can meet in happy harmony. For long-term success, the Cancer-Libra match must be built on kindness, trust, and loyalty. Both Cancer and Libra are also extremely sentimental, so once they create memories together, they're likely to form an unbreakable bond.

Cancer and Scorpio

When water and water meet, the results are...well, wet. Lunar Cancer is an extremely sensitive creature, so she needs to establish trust and loyalty before revealing her vulnerabilities. Accordingly, like-minded Scorpio makes a terrific partner for the delicate crab. This connection is built on deep intuition and psychic skills, so Cancer and Scorpio can often communicate through nonverbal (maybe even telepathic) forms of expression. Sure, both Cancer and Scorpio can be extremely moody (with so many emotions, what else would you expect?!), but they know how to support each other, illuminating the path forward even in one partner's darkest hours. Fundamentally, both Cancer and Scorpio are looking for the same things: privacy, fidelity, and intimacy. This is surely a match made in the stars (or, in the case of these water signs, the ocean).

Cancer and Sagittarius

This alignment isn't *impossible*...but fair warning, it's not going to be easy. At first, each of these two extremely different energies may be attracted to the other's differences: fast-talking Sagittarius is empowered by Cancer's nurturing spirit, while the celestial crab is hypnotized by the archer's effortless finesse. But fundamentally, Sagittarius's need to explore doesn't mesh well with Cancer's domestic desires. After all, how can Cancer build a safe and secure nest if her partner is always running away? In a Cancer-Sagittarius couple, Cancer must remember that home isn't a place; it's a state of mind. Likewise, Sagittarius will need to realize that stability does *not* mean confinement. If these two are willing to alter their perceptions just a bit, there is a lot of hope for the Cancer-Sagittarius match.

When Stars Align

Ready for a ride? Even if Cancer and Sagittarius can't link up long term, the celestial crustacean should enjoy a wild date with this brazen stallion *at least* once. Who knows—they may end up eloping by the shore!

Cancer and Capricorn

Although they are astrological opposites, Cancer and Capricorn share similar values: both care deeply about their family members and friends, and also about the building of a sustainable future. Though seemingly less emotional than Cancer, hardworking Capricorn deeply appreciates Cancerian sensitivities. Meanwhile, Cancer's intuition can bring some much-needed spirituality to Capricorn's practicality. The Cancer-Capricorn relationship is perfect for cohabitation, as both signs enjoy nesting and building safe spaces. However, since they both also fear change, Cancer and Capricorn must work hard to make sure their relationship doesn't become stale. After all, you don't need to snuggle up by the fire *every* night of the week; it's okay to have some fun outside of the home every once in a while too!

Cancer and Aquarius

Though this bond seems odd at first (Cancer is quite traditional, whereas Aquarius is extremely progressive), both signs are actually innovative thinkers with bright ideas for how to live creatively and impactfully in the world. Their perspectives are extremely dissimilar, however. Cancer's opinions always reflect her immediate realities, whereas Aquarius theorizes at 30,000 feet above the ground. As a result, there can be some discord within a Cancer-Aquarius partnership: Aquarius doesn't understand why Cancer personalizes everything, and Cancer feels hurt by Aquarius's clinical aloofness. The Cancer-Aquarius partnership needs to work hard to ensure that each partner's distinct needs are being satisfied. Through time and open dialogue, this unlikely pair might have the potential to build a long-lasting bond.

Cancer and Pisces

In a Cancer-Pisces relationship, the celestial crab may finally meet her emotional match. Crustaceans divide their time between living in the water (symbolizing the emotional world) and living on the shore (symbolizing the physical world). Likewise, while Cancer is often moody, her sensitivities are environmentally based: she is simply responding to whatever is happening in her physical reality. Pisces, on the other hand, is a deep-sea fish. This aquatic creature never comes up for air, so she is constantly living in her emotional domain. When bonded with Pisces, Cancer has her work cut out for her; though she can meet Pisces at the shore, she'll drown if she follows her too deep into the ocean! Accordingly, it's very important for Cancer to establish boundaries in a Cancer-Pisces pairing. Pisces will also need to do her part in making sure that the relationship doesn't become flooded with *too* many feelings. At the end of the day, however, water and water flow effortlessly together, and the Cancer-Pisces bond is extraordinarily magical.

When Stars Align

Between Cancer and Pisces, there is an entire oceanic ecosystem—but that doesn't mean these two need to spend all of their time submerged! Cancer and Pisces are both incredibly creative, so they can use their shared emotional gifts to make art (they should just be sure that it's appreciated on land!). In fact, these two could be the next Johnny Cash (Pisces) and June Carter Cash (Cancer)!

Love Planets: Venus and Mars

Though your Sun sign helps you understand your essence (your desires, needs, unique qualities, etc.), which is extremely important in exploring romantic compatibility, it is just one component of your rich, complex astrological profile. The placement of the planets Venus and Mars in your birth chart (a snapshot of the sky at your exact moment of birth) will also reveal critical information about your romantic sensibilities. In astrology, Venus is linked to love, beauty, and money. Simply put, Venus can help you understand the way you idealize partnership and approach your relationships. Mars governs ambition, momentum, and sex. When exploring romantic compatibility, it's important to examine the role of Mars within your astrological profile, as its placement will reveal insights into how you like to "get down." And honestly, whether a relationship lasts for one night or for an entire lifetime, sexual attraction is a major part of the equation.

Venus in Cancer

Venus in Cancer gravitates toward stable, reliable partnerships. In many ways, Venus's placement in Cancer is the most traditional application of this sensual planet. Venus in Cancer doesn't want to be wined and dined; she wants to be nurtured and protected. Since Cancer needs to be cajoled from her shell, Venus in Cancer is happiest in partnerships she perceives as safe and secure. Here, romance is all about domesticity.

Mars in Cancer

Mars is about action, determination, and motivation. Cancer is also extremely ambitious—but only when she feels supported. Thus, Mars in Cancer requires lots of positive feedback when being intimate, which isn't always easy...especially since people offer praise in many different ways. If you are in a partnership with Mars in Cancer—whether long-term or late-night—don't be afraid to offer genuine encouragement. Let her know that you enjoy her fancy moves and kinky experimentation! She'll appreciate the feedback and will be sure to continue delivering a show of dynamic bravado with pleasure.

Leo

(July 23–August 22)

Have you ever dated a Leo? You would definitely know: symbolized by the lion, this fiery wildcat will *not* let you forget his mighty roar. Ruled by the sun, Leo is always the center of his solar system...and he expects to be the star of his partner's galaxy as well. Although he typically has a cheery disposition, he also has a fierce bite to go along with his roar. Drama is infused in everything Leo does, so when he is angry, it's best to step out of his way.

The Celebrity Lifestyle

When Leo arrives, expect an entrance. He'll have already been through hair and makeup, so you'll need to be prepared with a red carpet, photographers, and *lots* of public adoration. The lion is the king of the celestial jungle—and he's delighted to embrace his royal status. In fact, Leo perceives himself as a royal celebrity. Dynamic, theatrical, and passionate, Leo loves to bask in the spotlight and honor...well, himself.

Written in the Stars

Leo's mythological origins go back quite a ways. Some scholars believe that the connection between the celestial constellation and the lion began over five thousand years ago in ancient Egypt.

The lion is also a natural leader, so he enjoys creating community. He cultivates friendships and romances that are artistically inspired. A shared love for museums, carefully curated playlists, and the theater sets Leo's heart aflame! But one of the lion's *favorite* types of creative dynamic is that fueled by drama. In fact, playful Leo actually adores drama-fueled romances that are suited for the tabloids. Get ready for reality TV–style blowouts that dissolve into passionate lovemaking! According to this astrological grandstander, passion requires a little fire (it is his natural element, after all). So, if you're trying to tame a lion, you also need to be ready to fight for his affection.

Despite his theatrics, however, as a fixed sign (born in the height of summer), Leo is renowned for his stability and loyalty. After all, the sun never goes retrograde. Leo is a dedicated partner who puts his heart into every relationship (fittingly, in medical astrology, Leo rules the heart). What you see is what you get with this lion. Of course, he can also be incredibly stubborn, but obstinance is always a reflection of dependability.

Written in the Stars

Although Leo is extremely active, this wildcat also needs sleep—and lots of it! Just as lions in the jungle oscillate between bursts of energy and extreme exhaustion, Leo requires plenty of rest. Don't be surprised if your lion partner loves to sleep late: for this feline, nothing is more luxurious than spending a lazy afternoon snuggling in bed.

Leo's Kingdom

Although Leo holds court, this sign *always* roots for the underdog. Leo hates mean-spirited bullying, and will always advocate on behalf of others. Indeed, the lion loves to watch his mates succeed—until he feels threatened by their power. When Leo leads with confidence, this sign is kind, generous, and thoughtful. A supported Leo will welcome an outsider with a loving warmth, and he will do whatever it takes to blanket that person's world with happiness and—perhaps more importantly—fun. It's crucial to note that Leo *loves* a good time: even in the darkest hour, a great party will always cheer up this jovial creature.

Written in the Stars

Leo is interested in money, but chiefly for the luxury that it can offer. After all, he wants his kingdom to be adorned! When Leo finally reaches the pinnacle of his success and feels financially secure, however, he is extremely philanthropic and will be delighted to give back to his community.

When Leo does feel that his crown is in jeopardy, though, he can become impaired by his ego and feelings of jealousy. Ultimately, his hubris is the greatest threat to his joy. In truth, his light can *never* actually be eclipsed: its radiance is eternal. Thus, another person's glow will never compromise his kingdom—if only he could remember this.

Written in the Stars

When Leo is entertaining—whether on stage or at a happy hour—he's "on." Don't forget, as long as there's an audience, everything is a performance for this dynamic fire sign. Unless you're planning on joining his act, don't you dare try to redirect the spotlight. Nothing makes Leo angrier than being upstaged.

The Sensitive Lion: Leo Quirks

Though Leo is inspired by drama, this sign is also deeply sensitive. Whether or not the tears are rooted in performance is irrelevant: of all the fire signs (Aries, Leo, and Sagittarius), Leo is definitely the most emotional. Leo gets his feelings hurt extremely easily, so his partner will need to know when (and how) to nurture this delicate creature. Loyalty is of the utmost importance to Leo, so when you've entered his kingdom, he requires unconditional love. A word to the wise: when this feline *does* have his feelings hurt, it's best not to offer advice. Leo is looking for comfort, not counsel, and will subsequently feel betrayed by his mate should they start giving their objective opinion on the situation.

Leo doesn't *always* have to be right about everything—but in order to get a word in edgewise, you will definitely need to prove your point. Leo will push you to the limit because he actually loves to be challenged. As long as your arguments are rooted in passion, bring on the paparazzi-worthy drama! Fur will be flying, but don't forget his sensitivity. The regal lion must also remember that partnerships aren't just for the tabloids; they also require an entire behind-the-scenes production. Compromise, dedication, and genuine vulnerability will help take Leo's bond to the next level, securing his partner a permanent role in his royal palace.

Zodiac Royalty: Attracting Leo

From a young age, Leo knows that he is zodiac royalty. Even the most reserved lion will have a regal air. So how do you impress a monarch? Compliment his kingdom, of course! This astrological attention-seeker never gets tired of praise, and lavish dinners, exclusive parties, and decadent designer wear will all make him feel adored. When pursuing him, keep in mind that it's not easy to keep up with this wildcat. In fact, sometimes it can be downright difficult to date a sign with such high standards. But it's certainly worthwhile in the end. Once you reserve your spot beside Leo, you definitely will not want to give up the throne.

Lessons in Love: What Should You Gift Leo?

Leo is associated with gold. In fact, the alchemy symbol for this vivid metal is the same symbol that represents the sun: a circle with a dot in the center. For thousands of years, gold has been linked to this vibrant star. For a birthday or anniversary, treat your Leo partner to a gold-toned gift: he'll feel like true royalty.

Finding His Co-Ruler

Leo doesn't mind a bit of ego in a partner. In fact, the lion wants to make sure that his mate is proud and confident. Of course, Leo isn't looking for a narcissist—pomposity is a total turnoff—but this bold creature must ensure his partner can wear a crown well. After all, Leo values the concept of a power couple, with his partner serving as an extension of himself. Since this fire sign is known for his bravado in everything, from his creative enterprises to his cinematic romances, it is *very* important that he aligns with someone who can serve up exactly what he is seeking.

Written in the Stars

Leo's day should be full, with not a moment wasted. This sunny lion wants to live life to its fullest; lack of fulfillment—either professionally or personally—could totally cloud his personality. If your Leo partner is in a rut, plan an exciting weekend filled with lots of magical activities and a reservation at an exclusive restaurant to top it off.

Royal Coitus

When it comes to sex, fiery Leo can also shine between the sheets. All in all, the biggest sexual turn-on for the lion is to *feel* desired. He is enchanted by seduction—both given and received. Affection should be displayed through lavish dates and grandiose romantic gestures. Ever bought someone twelve dozen roses? Well, if you're serious about Leo, it's time to find a great florist. This feline purrs at the idea of being desired, especially when that burning thirst results in passionate, filmic lovemaking.

Leo rules the heart and spine, so light caresses down your lion lover's back will get this erotic wildcat *extremely* aroused. To further spice things up, Leo and his lover should explore seated positions in chairs (ahem, thrones). These poses are perfect for him to share tender kisses—while also providing his theatrical moment in the spotlight (perhaps even sneaking in a quick lap dance).

Roaring Proudly: Maintaining a Relationship with Leo

On a good day, Leo is a warm, generous, and compassionate mate who radiates his positive energy toward his partner. On a bad day, however, he can become jealous, possessive, or even controlling. Leo must remember that relationships are about reciprocity: his partner also deserves to glow! If Leo isn't capable of sharing the stage, he may obscure his partner's unique radiance and damage the relationship.

> **Written in the Stars**
> Leo is extremely loyal—especially to those who have proven their unconditional commitment. Even if you're not ready to say "I do," small gestures to show Leo that you care deeply for him (for instance, unexpected romantic texts or thoughtful gifts) will go a long way with this big-hearted lion.

When a flame begins to dim and Leo senses that a relationship is spiraling downward, he tries to protect his pride by facilitating a quick, clean split. When in charge, he can usually bounce back fairly quickly from breakups. The truth is, this fiery lion is always falling in love. Leo likes his romances to be as big as his personality, and nothing makes him purr like unabashed adoration.

He needs to feel like he is the center of attention, and accordingly he may be seduced by dark, dangerous romances. Usually he is not interested in straying from a relationship—until someone expresses their attraction: after all, the "celebrity" is simply engaging his "fan." It's not easy for Leo to reject praise, so he gravitates toward this applause.

However, if the drama gets cut off early and Leo gets dumped, it's a *whole* different story. At first, his reaction to an unexpected split is often complete shock: "How could someone possibly lose interest in me?" After this phase, Leo then experiences devastating anguish. A breakup is a totally heart-wrenching experience, and this lion definitely showcases his suffering (watch out for lots of somber social media posts). Though other signs may perceive a grief-stricken Leo's behavior as over-the-top, his pain is genuine. But despite how dark things may get, the celestial lion is a resilient creature who will always find his way back to the light. In tarot, Leo is represented by the Strength card, which symbolizes physical, mental, and emotional fortitude. A fearless optimist who refuses to accept defeat, Leo can tap into deep wells of this strength, enabling him to always maintain his luminosity.

Sun Sign Love Matches

Leo always looks for a mate who excites his spirit—after all, the lion hates boredom. In fact, if Leo doesn't have enough stimulation to keep busy, he may gravitate toward dark and dangerous romances that offer cheap thrills. So, how can you tell if it's real love or just steamy infatuation? Explore the following matches to find out how this regal creature interacts with each of the twelve zodiac signs.

Leo and Aries

When fire and fire team up, it's not easy to contain the flames. These signs feed off of each other, creating a passionate partnership that is built on desire, determination, and panache. Ruled by the sun, Leo shines brightly when paired with Aries, a like-minded fire sign who gladly embraces Leo's magnetic charisma. Aries, who also requires lots of affection, is comforted by his lion partner's loyalty and warmth. However, while both Aries and Leo are confident, their exuberance manifests very differently: Leo always wears his heart on his sleeve, while Aries's primary concern is coming out on top. Although these powerhouses bring out the best in each other, they also need to keep their egos in check. Otherwise, the Leo-Aries bond may ultimately burn itself out.

Leo and Taurus

Though Leo and Taurus are both loyal and dedicated individuals, their pride and stubbornness can sometimes lead to major clashes. Taurus is put off by Leo's ostentation, and the lion finds himself growling at the bull's unapologetic obstinance. When coupled, both Leo and Taurus need to make sure their motives aren't excessively self-interested, instead adopting a more easygoing attitude to ensure a partnership that is equally balanced. After all, Leo and Taurus actually have a lot in common: both love the finer things in life (expensive wine, chic restaurants, and designer threads). So, if these two can focus more on their similarities than their differences, they will be sure to enjoy a fun, supportive, and—perhaps most importantly—superglamorous partnership.

When Stars Align

Both Taurus and Leo love nice things—but both are also extremely possessive. To ensure a healthy relationship between these two hardheaded signs, neither should count on sharing. This may cost more up front (obviously it would be cheaper to not buy two of everything), but in the end the bond will definitely yield a return on investment.

Leo and Gemini

At first, a Leo-Gemini bond is sexy and carefree. Leo needs to feel like a VIP, and somehow, Gemini always has tickets to the hottest party in town. At the end of the night, however, Leo wants to let down his mane and snuggle up to a cuddly, loyal partner. Unfortunately, Gemini may not be able to serve that role: the celestial twin is still out partying! In a Leo-Gemini relationship, both individuals need to learn how to accommodate the other's needs. Leo must trust Gemini's nonstop socializing, and Gemini must honor Leo's request for emotional fidelity. When these two can compromise, however, this match is dynamic, playful, and very sexually charged.

Leo and Cancer

It's not always easy for neighboring zodiac signs to date. If you think about it spatially, signs that sit so close together sometimes just don't have a lot of perspective. Likewise, a Leo-Cancer relationship isn't particularly easy for *either* person: Leo feels stifled by Cancer's moodiness, and Cancer resents Leo's over-the-top dramatics. If these two are committed to making their relationship work, however, they will need to bond over their shared values: loyalty, family, and honesty. Leo and Cancer also have the potential to uplift each other, helping the other reach their highest potential through genuine encouragement. It may not be without conflict, but when this partnership reaches an agreement, each sign will definitely stick to the terms.

Leo and Leo

Roll out the red carpet: the zodiac's most regal power couple has arrived! Leo loves to celebrate his radiance, so when two lions link up, they'll actually spend the majority of their relationship talking about the incredible gift of their bond (it may seem hyperbolic, but it's true). The Leo-Leo combo is a dramatic whirlwind that's destined to be filled with laughs, loyalty, and lots of adoration. But no kingdom is perfect, and since Leo has a pretty spectacular ego, expect competition—and lots of it. Whether they're fighting for the spotlight, microphone, or applause, their mutual need for praise could cause a strain on the relationship. The lion can be soothed, however, so to make a Leo-Leo bond last, each should be sure to stroke the other's mane often and carve out time for plenty of fiery passion.

Leo and Virgo

Though this is at first an unlikely pairing, fiery Leo and idealistic Virgo can actually bring out positive qualities in each other. Each sign should be aware though that this bond will require lots of understanding, tolerance, and—perhaps most importantly—honesty. At first, Virgo admires Leo's extravagance and effortless social finesse. Leo basks in this adoration—until the glow starts to fade. Virgo has a habit of idealizing, but since nothing in life is perfect, this earth sign can quickly become disenchanted with Leo's flamboyance. In order for a Leo-Virgo couple to work long term, it is important for each sign to make sure they are entering the relationship for the right reason, ensuring that the bond is not driven by ego.

Leo and Libra

The Leo-Libra alignment is dynamic: when coupled, the exuberant Leo and elegant Libra bring their best qualities to the table. Together, they're extremely social and endlessly entertained—attributes that are steadied thanks to Libra's exceptional gift for balance. However, since Libra is all about keeping the peace, he tends to be quite indecisive. Leo demands fearless loyalty, so Libra's apprehension can be frustrating for his Leo partner. Meanwhile, Libra can feel a bit smothered by Leo's possessiveness. If they can reconcile their differences, however, Leo and Libra will enjoy their shared appreciation for music, art, and luxury. At the end of the day, these two make a superb (and extremely well-dressed!) pair.

When Stars Align

Leo doesn't want to be liked; he wants to be *adored.* The lion won't waste his time building relationships with people who don't understand him, which could create tension with Libra, who always wants to keep the peace between his friends.

Leo and Scorpio

Although fire energy can sometimes feel limited by water (water is used to put out flames, after all), the Leo-Scorpio relationship is a power match. Both fixed signs, Leo and Scorpio have firm beliefs and uncompromising points of view. As a result, there is a palpable tension between these two, which can lead to some frustrating arguments—and, perhaps more importantly, incredible sex. Leo is particularly beguiled by Scorpio's dark and mysterious nature, while Scorpio is stimulated by Leo's warm radiance. However, it will take these two time to establish trust and understanding. Since both Leo and Scorpio have such different ways of moving through the world, they each need to learn how to understand the other's perspective. Once trust is established, however, neither Leo nor Scorpio will *ever* want to let go.

Leo and Sagittarius

Leo is drawn to Sagittarius like a moth to a flame. As the second fire sign, Leo's own flame is blazing, but contained (think of a bonfire). He just needs an audience. Sagittarius, on the other hand, knows no bounds. As the third and final fire sign of the zodiac, Sagittarius's energy is that of a roaring wildfire—requiring plenty of space to roam. Accordingly, Leo often gravitates toward this larger-than-life sign, looking up to him in aspirational awe. Sagittarius also appreciates Leo's glow, though in this bond he *always* makes a point to emphasize his freedom. If these two can reconcile the different ways they radiate their heat, their bond will be extremely charged. A Leo-

Sagittarius couple can spend hours chatting, laughing, and charming each other with dynamic stories and witty conversation.

When Stars Align

Leo is a hopeless romantic, so he will plan exciting, lavish adventures with Sagittarius: skiing in the Swiss Alps, yachting on the Mediterranean, taking an evening stroll in Paris... But what Leo will soon discover is that Sagittarius prefers a much more rugged approach to globe-trotting: more hostels than hotels.

Leo and Capricorn

Capricorn and Leo are different creatures: serious Capricorn focuses her energy on long-term achievements, whereas Leo is driven by fame and fortune. Surprisingly, however, Leo and Capricorn are an excellent romantic match. Both signs are extremely ambitious, so although they have different methodologies, they respect each other's motivation. And though these two will butt heads from time to time, the arguments will be predominately circumstantial (Leo, for instance, will want to stay out late singing karaoke, while Capricorn will want to go home early to finish an important project). When they work together, Leo and Capricorn can achieve greatness. Capricorn teaches Leo accountability, and Leo teaches Capricorn the art of a good time. If they invest fully in their relationship, there will definitely be a major return.

When Stars Align

At first, there can be a bit of tension between these two: Leo lives for the stage and Capricorn...well, she built the theater. When they team up, however, they make an unstoppable power couple. Think Barack Obama (Leo) and Michelle Obama (Capricorn), and Iman (Leo) and David Bowie (Capricorn). These are two serious duos!

Leo and Aquarius

Leo's opposite sign, Aquarius, is an interesting match for the royal lion. While Leo symbolizes the ruler, Aquarius represents the people. When coupled, they can create a system of checks and balances for each other that is driven by fairness and progressive thought. On a good day, the Leo-Aquarius bond exists in a beautiful, abundant kingdom. On a bad day, however, Aquarius perceives Leo as a selfish ruler, and Leo resents Aquarius's relentless subversion. In a Leo-Aquarius match, both partners need to work hard to understand the other's perspective. In order to do this successfully, Leo must dial down his ego and Aquarius must rev up his compassion. This bond has incredible potential, so healthy compromise will surely be rewarded.

Leo and Pisces

The Leo-Pisces bond is extremely unique. Leo (governed by the sun) is happiest when he can freely emanate his warm, radiant light. Pisces (the last sign of the zodiac) is connected to the sea, and just as the ocean reflects sunlight on the horizon, Pisces is happy to embrace—even enhance—Leo's vibrant glow. However, the ocean is a vast and mysterious place: beneath the surface there is little light, as the darkness absorbs it. While a Leo-Pisces bond can be powerful and seductive, it's important that the regal lion doesn't get swallowed by Pisces's extreme sensitivities. To ensure a happy relationship, these two must work hard to embrace each other's strongest qualities, celebrating their differences with kind appreciation and genuine respect.

Love Planets: Venus and Mars

Your Sun sign helps you understand your desires, needs, and special traits, which are extremely important in exploring romantic compatibility. However, this sign is just one part of your rich astrological profile. The birth chart (a snapshot of the sky at your exact moment of birth) features a number of planets—each with its own functions and purposes. Of these, Venus and Mars reveal critical information about your romantic sensibilities. The planet Venus is linked to love, beauty, and money. You can look to Venus to understand the way you idealize partnership, thus unlocking a deeper understanding of how you approach relationships. Mars, meanwhile, governs ambition, momentum, and sex. When exploring romantic compatibility, it's important to look at the placement of Mars within your birth chart. This placement will reveal critical insight into your preferences when it comes to physical intimacy. And, let's be honest, whether a relationship lasts one night or a lifetime, sexual attraction is a key part of the equation.

Venus in Leo

Romantic and passionate, Venus shines in Leo's vibrant domain. Simply put, Venus in Leo *loves* to be in love. Regal and generous, he will always worship (and be worshipped by) his partners. He idealizes the concept of a power couple—after all, he is constantly seeking a co-ruler for his kingdom. For Venus in Leo, a partnership is also personal, because he sees it as a reflection of his own identity. So, when he feels rejected, proceed with caution: there is a lot of ego embedded in romance, so a jilted Venus in Leo can quickly become ferocious.

Mars in Leo

Mars is a planet of drive and determination. The fire that fuels action, it shifts your spirit into high gear. Thus, Mars in Leo is aggressive and bodacious. This placement isn't afraid to get things done! Mars in Leo is more than willing to go above and beyond in his efforts—however, you must expect a healthy dose of ego. For this reason, while Mars in Leo is extremely motivated and ambitious, he will also expect acknowledgment for his efforts. So, when it comes to sex, make sure he gets *plenty* of positive reinforcement: let him know what you like! When Mars in Leo feels accomplished, this passionate lover will be sure to rise to the occasion again and again.

Chapter 6

Virgo

(August 23–September 22)

An earth sign, Virgo is represented by the goddess of agriculture: the virgin (an association that speaks to Virgo's deep roots in the material world). Virgo is practical and systematic in her approach to life. A perfectionist at heart, she seeks to improve herself and her skills through diligent and consistent practice—a trait that makes her one of the best partners of the zodiac.

The Mercurial Spirit

Virgo is governed by Mercury, the messenger planet of communication and travel. Interestingly, Mercury also rules Gemini, although these two signs are radically different: Gemini (an air sign) is about outward expression, whereas Virgo (an earth sign) is about internal processing. Simply put, Virgo is the "computer" of the zodiac: this incredible analyzer can transform even the most jumbled sets of information into organized, clear concepts—and express these concepts in a way that makes sense.

Virgo's desire to create logical systems aids her understanding of the world, but it also is intended to help others. In fact, this thoughtful sign is among the most dutiful of the zodiac. Virgo prides herself on being useful, so a huge component of her motivation is her ability to uplift others through kind acts of service. Think of Mother Teresa, Warren Buffett, and Tarana Burke. All of these quintessential Virgos dedicated their lives to giving back to the world in meaningful ways. Virgo makes a particularly phenomenal teacher and healer. Her skill in problem-solving enables her to help anyone who is struggling, from a student to a therapy client. Also possessing an incredible work ethic, Virgo applies clever ingenuity and a productive spirit to everything she touches (hello, Beyoncé!).

Unsurprisingly, Virgo is a thoughtful and caring partner, and she attracts others through her genuine kindness, striking intelligence, and empathetic compassion.

While this may all seem so effortless, a big part of the equation is the fact that Virgo holds herself to incredibly high standards. Virgo longs to be perfect in all pursuits and is always working to improve each and every thing she sets her mind to.

The Sharp Mind

Virgo is an intellectual: clever words, inspiring ideas, and clear communication are total aphrodisiacs to this earth sign. A big part of her intellectualism stems from her being so analytical and skilled at organizing concepts. Fueled by her love for collecting information, Virgo is usually an avid reader, movie buff, or music aficionado. As a mutable sign (born at the transition from the summer season), she is also extremely open-minded—a trait that often manifests in her artistic tastes. Virgo appreciates art that falls into lots of different genres and loves being introduced to new authors, movies, and songs.

Lessons in Love: Why Is *My* Virgo So Messy?

Virgo may be extremely meticulous about everything—but that doesn't mean she's always neat and tidy. In fact, some of the *messiest* people are Virgos! Why? Well, everyone manifests energy differently. While some Virgos may focus on organizing their possessions, others channel their energy toward their interpersonal dynamics, categorizing their friendships, and figuring out how each person fits neatly into their life.

Since Virgo relies on logic and organization, when it comes to matters of the heart, this mercurial sign seeks a partner who aligns with her day-to-day life. Do you both shower in the morning as opposed to at night? Do you have similar sleep schedules? Do you enjoy starting Sunday mornings with a crossword puzzle? Virgo uses data to create a complete profile of her partner, family members, and friends: every single person in her life—along with their habits, likes, and dislikes—is stored into a mental folder.

The Perfectionist: Virgo Quirks

Above all else, Virgo truly wants to help. Through her supportiveness, resourcefulness, and practicality, this earth sign is always striving to provide workable solutions to broken systems—but she should be careful. Though Virgo's critical thinking is her greatest strength, it can also be a weakness when it comes to her relationships. When this energy is not effectively managed, Virgo's desire for perfection within herself can be projected onto those around her. Her observations shift from thoughtful and astute to overly critical and nitpicky.

For healthy relationships, Virgo must remain nonjudgmental and allow her loved ones to pursue their own ways of doing things. She should also remember that constantly chasing after perfection within herself can become destructive. In fact, there is beauty *within* imperfection, so it's important for Virgo to learn to recognize that what she views as a flaw can be an advantage, rather than a defect. For example, her attention to detail (which she may see as debilitating) makes her one of the most discerning signs of the zodiac. She can quickly cut through layers of artifice to understand the truth of a situation.

Acts of Kindness: Attracting Virgo

Virgo is attracted to intellect. Since she is the most analytical sign of the zodiac, it's no surprise that the fastest way into her heart is through her mind. In fact, when Virgo finds a compatible partner, the mental sparks are electric: you can hear the neurons firing off (seriously—listen for them!). When she is interested in cultivating a new relationship, she showcases her curiosity through focus, patience, and practice; though she may not be the most direct about her intentions, you can always tell that Virgo is romantically interested if she tries to help you with a project. Likewise, one of the best ways to display your own affection for Virgo is to lend a hand. Simple things—like picking up her dry-cleaning, feeding her pet, or running a quick errand—will demonstrate that you're an excellent partner for kind Virgo and will leave this sweet earth sign completely smitten.

Written in the Stars

Although Virgo doesn't require applause (save the clapping for Leo, Virgo's astrological neighbor), she does want to be acknowledged for her achievements. She may not directly ask for praise, but be sure to always express your gratitude for Virgo's generosity. It will mean more to her than you could ever imagine.

Sexual Healing

In traditional astrology, the idyllic virgin represents the Virgo constellation—a mythology that often leads to the false assumption that Virgo is innocent and chaste. In reality, this is *far* from accurate. It is true that, when it comes to sex, this sign has a youthful energy—but she is more hormonal than she is naive.

Governed by Mercury, there's an inquisitive nature to her sexuality; she fixates on nearly every aspect of getting down, including contemplating who around her is having sex and with whom. Indeed, you'll know your Virgo lover feels comfortable with you when she starts asking a *ton* of questions about your sexual history. These conversations may feel a bit awkward at first, but it's actually a huge turn-on to this communication-centric sign (remember, Virgo is ruled by the planet of expression). She will store all of your kinks and fantasies, and she will be sure to incorporate them into your future romantic trysts. For instance, if you *casually* mention that you are turned on by sexy underwear, don't be surprised if your Virgo partner suddenly has an entire closet filled with exotic bedtime wear.

Additionally, this intellectual sign is extremely aroused by witty humor and intelligent conversation. In theory, Virgo would be an incredible romance novelist, but if your Virgo lover *isn't* Nicholas Sparks or Jane Austen, she'll probably showcase this in short form. That's right: Virgo *loves* sexting.

Kinks and Snags

So, Virgo can talk the talk—but can this earth sign walk the walk? Don't be surprised if your Virgo lover is quite shy in the bedroom—at least in the beginning. Virgo is a creature of habit, so until she develops a dialogue, she'll be an observant lover who will be very aware of what motions turn on her partner.

That doesn't mean she's not kinky—in fact, Virgo *loves* to get freaky in the bedroom. Within a safe and secure environment, Virgo will want to have regular sex that allows her to explore all her proclivities. Just don't try to throw in something unexpected without warning: sudden shifts in rhythm or roles will throw Virgo off and send her straight back into her head. In order for Virgo to remain open and receptive, she needs to know what to expect from her partner. She should also consider reverse cowgirl–type positions: although this sign loves eye contact, having the opportunity to look away can actually give her the opportunity to focus on pleasure rather than observation, enabling her to really let loose. *Yee-haw!* Additionally, in medical astrology, Virgo is associated with the lower stomach. Titillate your Virgo lover by running your nails gently across her belly. The effects will undoubtedly be volcanic.

Keep It Simple: Maintaining a Relationship with Virgo

Since Virgo loves to be helpful and use her detail-oriented skills whenever possible, she can be prone to being so accommodating that she ends up as a sponge for other people's problems. The best way to combat this, of course, is to keep things clean and uncomplicated. Although your Virgo partner is compassionate, don't make her the keeper of all your problems. If you dump all of your stress on Virgo, she'll get overwhelmed. Instead, consider seeking other outlets for your frustrations.

Written in the Stars

Virgo governs the digestive system, so this sign is often very sensitive to food! She may have certain allergies or intolerances, so before you wine and dine your Virgo partner, make sure you know what she can and can't eat.

Don't Judge Me

Here's an important thing to remember when it comes to a lasting relationship with Virgo: she will be dependable, but she will also need to count on you too—especially when she accidentally tightens the wrong screw in her quest to fix things. However, don't even *think* about criticizing Virgo's scrutiny. It may seem ironic, but Virgo hates being called out for her detail-oriented behavior. She is extremely sensitive about this aspect of her personality, so when in doubt, just let her do her thing—even if that means taking a step back. This will allow her to actually come to *you* for help, deepening your bond tremendously.

Written in the Stars

Virgo loves to fix things—a habit that often leads her to attract unavailable people. It's important for Virgo to remember that she cannot repair what was never working: toxic relationships have no antidote.

The Virgo Ghost

Because Virgo strives for a near-impossible ideal in everything, including romance, when the fantasy of perfection finally fades, she will have already completely checked out of the relationship—with or without informing her partner. But she doesn't mean to be malicious. Gentle Virgo just hates letting people down and, accordingly, will attempt to leave a relationship without having a difficult discussion. In other words, Virgo (along with the other mutable signs of Gemini, Sagittarius, and Pisces) is extremely guilty of "ghosting"—or disappearing without a trace. If you do manage to get in contact with your Virgo partner *before* she reaches the "other side," she will be extremely apologetic. In fact, she'll try to alleviate the tension by assuming total responsibility, proclaiming some version of "it's not you, it's me." In Virgo's mind, the faster she can complete the conversation, the better.

On the other hand, when a breakup takes Virgo by surprise, this earth sign has a much more difficult time letting go. She'll play every detail of the relationship back in her head over and over again in an attempt to discover the *precise* point things took a turn for the worse.

And, naturally, Virgo wants what she can't have (hey, she's only human), so she will have carefully constructed arguments detailing why her former partner was perfect in every way (even if she spent the majority of the relationship complaining about them). When dealing with heartbreak, Virgo must remember that her romantic decisions should be informed by a partnership's reality, not its idealized potential.

Sun Sign Love Matches

Though she is organized, logical, and extremely methodical, in a classic moment of cosmic irony, Virgo isn't always black-and-white. In fact, Virgo is an extremely complex creature. For instance, despite her "virginal" qualities, she shouldn't be misunderstood as being chaste by default. And if Virgo finds enough data points to conclude that her existing relationship is imperfect, she is happy to look elsewhere for a fulfilling bond. So, which partner signs are most compatible with this mercurial creature? In the following sections, you'll discover how Virgo relates romantically to each sign of the zodiac.

Virgo and Aries

Aries can talk a big game, but can he follow through? In a Virgo-Aries pairing, analytical Virgo will be sure to call BS on Aries's overly ambitious bragging. Aries, on the other hand, will be totally caught off guard by Virgo's incredible attention to detail. Within this bond, Aries will undoubtedly be held accountable for his actions. Of course, this may lead to some ego-bruising when Virgo sees the cracks in Aries's plans, so both Virgo and Aries must be willing to accept the occasional miscommunication (and temper tantrum on Aries's part). However, if Virgo can learn to accept Aries's shortsightedness, and Aries can work on releasing his pride, the Virgo-Aries partnership can be extremely valuable. A strong relationship between Virgo and Aries will be based in honesty, respect, and encouragement.

When Stars Align

Aries and Virgo don't always see eye to eye, but these two have incredible sexual chemistry. When linked, each sign infuses the bond with the sensual energy of their planetary ruler. Aries leads with passionate Mars, while Virgo spices it up with Mercury's alluring banter. The Aries-Virgo match is *all* about dirty talk!

Virgo and Taurus

Ruled by Mercury, Virgo is always processing information. She also prefers to communicate through linear, organized expression. This pragmatic sign feels extremely grounded when paired with earthy, sensual Taurus. Virgo is inspired by Taurus's effortless *joie de vivre*, and Taurus appreciates Virgo's analytical eye and attention to detail. Although the attraction is magnetic however, there are some significant differences between the two signs. Taurus's more hedonistic tendencies may make Virgo anxious, which—in turn—can make Taurus feel judged and unsafe. Thankfully, the easy alignment of these signs will outweigh the obstacles. The Virgo-Taurus match is a well-balanced relationship that is built on hard work, trust, and loyalty. When these two work together, anything is possible.

When Stars Align

As earth signs, Virgo and Taurus connect through rationality—but that doesn't mean they lack emotions! In their own ways, both Virgo and Taurus can be *totally* dramatic (Virgo gets caught up in nuance, while Taurus goes on a righteous rant). If, however, they can guide each other back to earth, they will always find stability.

Virgo and Gemini

Though this pair may seem a bit mismatched at first, introverted Virgo and outgoing Gemini actually have a lot in common. Both Virgo and Gemini are governed by Mercury (the planet of expression), so these two signs are deeply committed to the art of communication. Quick-witted Gemini loves to share, and clever Virgo is an astute observer who loves to process information. Though Gemini's signature flirtatious sensibilities make Virgo a *bit* uneasy, her romantic anxieties can be easily mitigated through honest and direct dialogue. If Gemini respects Virgo's needs—empathizing with the earth sign's more trepidatious temperament—the Virgo-Gemini bond can be extremely rewarding. Through this union, Gemini will become increasingly compassionate, and Virgo will learn how to have some fun (after all, not everything needs to be preplanned).

Virgo and Cancer

Individually, both Virgo and Cancer tend to overthink. Virgo gets caught up in minutiae, turning every situation into a worst-case scenario. Similarly, sensitive Cancer pays attention to subtle shifts in energy, noting even the smallest changes in body language or verbal intonation. On a bad day, Virgo and Cancer will feed each other's anxieties, inciting even more fear and paranoia. However, since they process stress so differently (earthy Virgo focuses on facts, and watery Cancer dwells on emotions), this relationship offers an opportunity for genuine healing, growth, and companionship. Virgo and Cancer encourage each other to look at their dilemmas from an alternative perspective, adding incredible multidimensionality to situations they may have viewed previously as being hopeless. These thoughtful signs are also extremely protective of each other, so when partnered, the Virgo-Cancer match is nurturing and supportive.

Virgo and Leo

Within the zodiac, each sign only contains as much information as its preceding signs. In other words, fiery Leo's spirit is an amalgamation of Aries, Taurus, Gemini, Cancer, and Leo energy. However, because each sign can't see past their own vista in the zodiac, they have no awareness of what's to come. Accordingly, the sign directly following your own is often considered your blind spot. In the case of Leo, this blind spot is Virgo. Virgo baffles Leo: this fire sign simply does not understand why Virgo is so risk-averse. Virgo, on the other hand, knows that life is much more complicated than just having fun: everything takes time, practice, and patience. Due to this dissonance, it's not always easy to navigate a Virgo-Leo bond. However, if each sign can approach the relationship with an open mind (and open heart), they will be able to form a long-lasting love that is inspiring, encouraging, and emotionally gratifying.

Virgo and Virgo

One of Virgo's most important (and distinctive) attributes is her selflessness. Simply put, Virgo loves to be helpful—especially in practical, tangible ways. When paired with another Virgo, however, this quality gets a bit distorted. In a romantic relationship, two Virgos will be trying to fix each other *constantly*, each convinced that their own, individual methodology is superior. In addition, since Virgo hates conflict, this tension may become increasingly passive-aggressive, resulting in lots of nitpicking and snippy comments. But don't worry: the Virgo-Virgo bond is not doomed. If these two signs explore the nuances of their individual strengths (for instance, one Virgo may be exceptionally tidy, while the other may be a brilliant copyeditor), they can identify the best ways to help each other in different situations. If the Virgo-Virgo couple leads with love instead of judgment, they can build a relationship that's supportive, caring, and intellectually stimulating.

Virgo and Libra

Although Virgo and Libra have different definitions of perfection, both of these signs are extremely idealistic. Virgo wants life to be organized and systematic, and Libra strives for balance and harmony. When coupled, the Virgo-Libra pair can merge their individual skills (Virgo is incredibly detail oriented, while Libra has an effortless aesthetic sensibility), building a relationship that is the paradigm of partnership. However, though both Virgo and Libra want a spotless bond, they must learn to accept that no relationship is without its flaws. In fact, some healthy conflict can actually *help* propel a relationship forward: friction can facilitate momentum. By accepting their imperfections, they can build a sustainable (and, perhaps more importantly, honest) union. After all, magic always exists within the cracks of truth.

When Stars Align

Virgo and Libra can certainly have their shortcomings as a couple, but one of the most magical things about this bond is each sign's ability to manifest their creativity. Between Virgo's attention to detail and Libra's effortless charm, these two have all the tools they need to turn their dreams into reality. Will Smith (Libra) and Jada Pinkett Smith (Virgo) are a classic example!

Virgo and Scorpio

There is no zodiac sign more closely linked to sex than Scorpio is: this passionate water sign is known for her erotic electricity. Virgo, on the other hand, has the opposite reputation. With a name derived from the mythological virgin archetype, Virgo is often perceived as chaste and prudish. It's time to scrap this outdated stereotype: Virgo loves to "get down." Consequently, the chemistry between Virgo and Scorpio is palpable. Virgo is enchanted by Scorpio's effortless sensuality, and Scorpio is intrigued by Virgo's unassuming allure. They instinctively know how to satisfy each other's carnal desires. Outside the bedroom, however, the Virgo-Scorpio pair must work a bit harder to maintain their spark. Virgo must avoid micromanaging Scorpio, and Scorpio must be willing to let down her guard. Through dedication and a little elbow grease, Virgo and Scorpio make an excellent match.

Virgo and Sagittarius

Virgo and Sagittarius are the funniest signs of the zodiac. Virgo's humor is driven by nuance, whereas Sagittarius's fiery vivacity fuels incredible storytelling. When paired, they form a comedy duo. But beyond Virgo's hilarious observations and Sagittarius's hardy laughter, this couple must work hard to ensure a healthy partnership. When Virgo's meticulousness takes a turn for the worse, she can become extremely nitpicky—which is problematic for adventurous Sagittarius, who believes that the little details are less important than the big picture. Meanwhile, Virgo perceives Sagittarius's behavior as reckless, growing increasingly frustrated by his cavalier attitude. For a Virgo-Sagittarius partnership to sustain, Sagittarius must find compassion for Virgo's fussiness, and Virgo must be willing to embrace Sagittarius's mischievous inclinations. If these two can work together, they will be sure to enjoy a playful dynamic filled with endless giggles.

Lessons in Love: How Do Mutable Signs Relate to Each Other?

The mutable signs—Gemini, Virgo, Sagittarius, and Pisces—are all extremely open-minded and adaptable, changing their minds frequently. When they partner, however, it can sometimes get slippery: because mutable energy is so fluid, in some partnerships it's not always easy for these signs to stick together!

Virgo and Capricorn

Virgo and Capricorn are a match made in the stars—or, for these two grounded signs, on earth. Both Virgo and Capricorn are earth signs that are ambitious, hardworking, and responsible. Capricorn values Virgo's analytical eye and attention to detail, while Virgo is enchanted by Capricorn's enterprising spirit and big-picture vision. However, because this relationship is so safe and sensible, both partners will need to work hard to prevent it from becoming overly methodical. In this case, bossy Capricorn may start to treat helpful Virgo like an assistant, which can make Virgo feel bitter and resentful. The Virgo-Capricorn pair should infuse spice into their relationship through exciting date nights, impromptu adventures, and other ways of breaking routine. As long as the Virgo-Capricorn bond doesn't get *too* comfortable, this relationship is built to last.

Virgo and Aquarius

Both Virgo and Aquarius are keenly aware of their external realities. These hyperanalytical signs love to explore systems, coloring their surroundings with astute observations and carefully crafted insights. Despite their mutual appreciation for observation, however, the ways in which Virgo and Aquarius process their surroundings couldn't be more different. Earthy Virgo is pragmatic; she pays close attention to tangible nuances and the small details. Aquarius, on the other hand, thinks about things on a global, societal level. There will be some tension between these signs (after all, Virgo hates breaking the rules, while

Aquarius is always trying to start a revolution), but if they can learn to work together, their combined perspectives will form a comprehensive view of the world. Adjustments will be necessary, but as a couple, Virgo and Aquarius have incredible potential.

Virgo and Pisces

Virgo and Pisces sit across from each other in the zodiac wheel; they're opposite signs that love to be helpful in different ways. Virgo represents "daytime magic," while Pisces represents "nighttime magic." In practice, this means that Virgo lends a hand in physical, pragmatic ways (she excels in gardening, fitness, or medicine), while Pisces's assistance is more abstract and spiritual (she is a skilled spiritual healer). Accordingly, Virgo and Pisces are both sensitive and compassionate individuals who relate to each other on a deeply empathetic level. Virgo's logical mind also helps wandering Pisces achieve her goals, while Pisces's creative ingenuity inspires Virgo to explore more artistic forms of self-expression. Although it's important for each sign to maintain her unique identity (boundaries are hard for these two), a Virgo-Pisces bond will bring out the best in each sign and, in doing so, create a truly enchanted union.

Love Planets: Venus and Mars

While your Sun sign helps you understand your essence (the sum of your desires, needs, and unique qualities), it is just one component of your rich astrological profile. The birth chart (a snapshot of the sky at your exact moment of birth) also features the planets of Venus and Mars, which reveal critical information about your romantic sensibilities. In astrology, Venus is linked to love, beauty, and money. Simply put, you can look to Venus to understand the way you idealize partnership and approach your relationships. Mars, meanwhile, governs ambition, momentum, and sex. When exploring romantic compatibility, it's important to look at the role of Mars within your astrological profile. Its placement will offer insights into your sexual likes and dislikes. And honestly, whether a relationship lasts one night or an entire lifetime, sexual attraction is a major piece of the puzzle.

Venus in Virgo

Venus in Virgo people love to problem-solve, and value partnerships based on reciprocity. Virgo's earthy energy is practical and organized, so when fused with sensual Venus, she is wooed by thoughtful acts of service. Small and subtle gestures—for instance, assisting with laundry or running errands—make Venus in Virgo's heart flutter. Though there is a lot of idealization embedded in her relationships (Virgo strives for perfection), for this sweet sign, there is truly nothing more romantic than when her partner lends a helping hand.

Mars in Virgo

Mars's energy is vibrant and impassioned. Virgo, on the other hand, is a bit more down-to-earth; this sign is cautious and analytical when it comes to decision-making. Accordingly, Mars in Virgo has a more subdued temperament. Under this sky, Mars no longer focuses on fighting; instead, the planet adopts an extremely meticulous sensibility. Mars in Virgo is systematic, linear, and detail oriented (this placement is excellent for copyeditors and lawyers). She is turned on by intelligence and humor, and although she can be a bit uptight (don't even *think* about having sex on dirty sheets), she is a gentle, loving, and dedicated partner.

Libra

(September 23–October 22)

Represented by the scales, Libra is obsessed with balance and strives to create equilibrium in all aspects of his life. As an air sign, he maintains the objectivity needed to always be fair through his open-mindedness, which also makes him the most socially fluid sign of the zodiac. Charming, and effortlessly popular among his peers, you can spot Libra seamlessly navigating happy hours, dinner parties, and casual hangouts.

The Aesthetic Judge

Libra is the true aesthete of the zodiac. Venus (the planet of love, beauty, and money) rules both Taurus and Libra, but Libra's relationship with Venus is a bit different than Taurus's. For Libra, his romantic nature is entirely cerebral: he adores high art, intellectualism, and connoisseurship. This dapper sign can be found sipping wine in a vineyard, applauding modern artwork at a gallery, or shopping for the latest designer threads. He also needs to surround himself with stunning objects that reflect his sophisticated interests and, accordingly, makes an excellent stylist and decorator.

Lessons in Love: Is Libra a Fair Judge?
Libra's symbol, the scales, is often used to represent the court system. Likewise, Libra prides himself on his objectivity. It's very important to him that he understand all sides of a situation and weigh each side evenly. When it comes to romance, however, Libra is not impartial: he has his own preferences, biases, and opinions, so don't be surprised if he tips the scales every so often.

But don't read Libra's elevated preferences as an indication of his disinterest in what lies beneath the surface. In fact, represented in tarot by the Justice card, Libra cares deeply about fairness and fighting on behalf of others for what is right. Thus, he will adopt the role of a wise and impartial judge whenever a situation calls for it. Of course, Libra would *never* be heavy-handed with his morals: this refined sign can effortlessly resolve conflicts by simply turning on the charm. His social finesse is *true* magic.

Finding Balance

Libra is represented by the air element. Air is a conduit: it breathes life into the three other astrological elements (fire, earth, and water) by enhancing their personal dispositions. Accordingly, while Libra's fiery opposite, Aries, represents *me*, Libra symbolizes *we*. Indeed, relationships are *paramount* for Libra, who finds balance in partnership. He loves harmonious bonds with fashionable mates... especially those who make attractive arm candy.

Written in the Stars

Libra is a cardinal sign (born at the start of fall), which means he is excellent at manifesting his desires—especially when it comes to harmony. Like the other cardinal signs (Aries, Cancer, and Capricorn), Libra can be a bit self-interested, but really, a *touch* of ego isn't a bad thing: confidence helps propel motion forward!

Simply put, this sign is just *happier* when coupled. However, in a monogamous partnership, Libra *must* be careful not to seek attention outside the agreed-upon boundaries of his bond. Since he likes to keep everyone happy and engaged, he may find himself tempted to push the limits of flirtation. On a bad day, Libra will stop at nothing to be well received by his peers—even if that means jeopardizing his existing relationships.

Lessons in Love: How Do You Stop Libra from Flirting?
You don't! Libra is extremely flirtatious! Keep in mind, however, that Libra's coquettish nature is *not* a reflection of his devotion. In fact, Libra is often an exceptionally loyal partner. If you get jealous easily, however, you'll need to consider whether pairing up with Libra is the right choice for you.

Weighing the Scales: Libra Quirks

As a cardinal sign, Libra is great at launching new initiatives and can see every possible option in a given situation. But, because he considers all of these perspectives in every pursuit, he also struggles with indecision. It's hard for him to make a choice, since he is constantly weighing the scales!

Written in the Stars
Libra has *such* a hard time making up his mind that sometimes he needs outside assistance to help him reach a conclusion. It may sound silly, but a coin toss is actually a great method for making a decision: if he is unhappy with the results, it means that his instinct was the alternative option (so he should go with it!).

In medical astrology, Libra governs the skin, and unsurprisingly, this air sign is also highly motivated by physical appearances. Vanity can definitely be a weakness for Libra, and he may become too focused on a partner fitting his desired aesthetic mold. However, good taste isn't always a bad thing: when coupled with Libra, you can be sure that you will *always* be the best-dressed pair at any party!

True Romance: Attracting Libra

The keyword with Libra is *refinement*, so he is turned off by those who come on too strong. Brash or stifling behavior (such as engaging in excessive texting or trying to define the relationship too early) is definitely going to send this air sign running for the hills. Instead, Libra wants a relationship that is sophisticated and unfolds organically: he and his partner should cultivate love and trust over time, forming a connection based on a shared interest in the finer things. To kick off a romance with Libra, consider attending a gallery opening or cocktails hour; when he sees how gracefully you move through different social situations, he'll be hooked!

Lessons in Love: How Do You Dress for a Date with Libra?

Presentation is extremely important to Libra, so do not show up to your first date dressed like a schlub. Some signs may not care about clothes (for instance, Capricorn isn't that interested in specific style choices), but for this cosmic aesthete, dirty old sneakers may very well be a deal breaker.

Since Libra loves to be in love, it's common to find him diving headfirst into romance. He is suave and debonair; between black-tie soirees, gallery excursions, and spontaneous trips to the countryside, dates with Libra can feel like a montage from your favorite romantic comedy. Indeed, this charming air sign *certainly* knows how to impress. But in these over-the-top displays of courtship, there's also a lot of projection. Libra has a very clear-cut view of what he wants, so it's easy for him to try to mold his mate to fit these desires, rather than consider that their own wants may be different. When bonding with Libra, he'll definitely know how to showcase perfection, but is he actually listening? The best way to tell whether Libra is truly investing in the connection is *not* through the obvious romantic gestures, but through the small, subtle moments of appreciation. When Libra is in love, he may end up replacing that $200 bottle of wine with a six-pack of inexpensive beer—not because he's being lazy or cheap, but because he's actually interested in what his partner prefers.

Written in the Stars

Did you know that Libra's lucky day is Friday? In traditional astrology, each planet is associated with a day of the week: Friday is linked to Venus, Saturday to Saturn, Sunday to the sun, and Monday to the moon. Since Venus governs Libra, this air sign shines the brightest on this day of the week!

Sexual Favors

When it comes to sex, Libra is obsessed with being courted, so although physical intimacy is important, this air sign needs a lot of mental foreplay leading up to the act. After a long night of wining and dining, your Libra lover will be excited to deepen the connection at home. That being said, don't even *think* about trying to get hot and heavy in an unaesthetic environment. While some signs may be totally aroused by the fantasy of spontaneous sexual encounters in restaurant bathrooms, elegant Libra finds these fiery trysts way too crass.

Between the sheets, Libra is extremely giving, so expect this Venusian lover to go above and beyond the call of duty. But don't be fooled by his generosity: he appreciates a highly reciprocal dynamic, so expect to return all favors. Specifically, take note of exactly how Libra is attending to you in bed; he will want the exact same attention...with accumulated interest, of course (after all, he *did* let you go first).

This air sign also rules the kidneys, so his lower back is quite the erogenous zone. Focus your hands here, and Libra will be totally enchanted. And when it comes to positions, what better embodies balanced Libra than the 69? Flip your Libra partner upside down and uncover the true meaning of harmony.

Tipping the Scales: Maintaining a Relationship with Libra

Libra is always seeking perfect balance: the peanut butter to his jelly, the yin to his yang. Since he is so obsessed with harmony, this air sign avoids conflict like the plague. At first, this peaceful disposition may seem ideal—but in fact, it can be the greatest pitfall to his partnerships.

To avoid disappointing his partners, he is known to resort to white lies and half-truths. It's important in these instances to remember that Libra's intention is not to be manipulative; he just doesn't want you to be upset with him. In turn, Libra himself must remember that the objective in life isn't to be liked by everyone (an impossible feat); it's to build honest relationships with the people who matter most. Further, healthy disagreements offer opportunities for both partners to grow, learn, and establish boundaries when needed. Ultimately, compromise requires an honest dialogue. Voicing his disagreement will also keep Libra from becoming passive-aggressive and bitter over time, as he will be confronting issues directly rather than pushing them aside until they are so overwhelming they can even lead to a breakup.

Still, Libra is no stranger to breakups: since he is happiest when coupled, it's no surprise that this air sign is often constantly moving in and out of relationships. In *his* perfect world, breakups wouldn't exist. Instead, partnerships would mimic his own airy essence, occurring in free-flowing states without clunky starts, stops, or formalities. The truth is, Libra likes to keep the door open. Even in a serious relationship, he may continue interacting with old flames. He understands that different relationships satisfy different needs, and until he knows exactly what he wants long term, he believes it's best to maintain his options by keeping *as many* doors open as possible.

When Libra does initiate a breakup, he often leads with agreeable, even ambiguous language (for example, saying "let's take a break" rather than "let's break up"). He always wants to keep the door open; as the resident peacekeeper of the zodiac, he never wants to make a hard and fast rule that could inadvertently create an enemy. And if he is on the receiving end of the split, he will do *everything* to make sure the partnership ends on good terms. After all, Libra cares deeply about the impressions he makes on others, so even after a romance is over, he would rather maintain a friendship with an ex than banish them forever. In the end, it's not just about romance—it's also about reputation.

Sun Sign Love Matches

Libra is extremely malleable, often happy to reflect his partner's sensibilities. Fittingly, he'll spread flames with fire signs, create waves with water signs, build mountains with earth signs, and fuel dynamic gusts of wind with like-minded air signs. Ultimately, Libra's goal is to create a balanced, beautiful life with his partner. So, how does Libra go about cultivating and maintaining harmony when matched with the different signs of the zodiac? Read on to find out!

Libra and Aries

Represented by the scales, Libra loves being in a pair. Accordingly, his opposite sign, Aries, makes for an interesting match. Aries is known for his fierce independence, so when these two signs pair up, they create an intriguing balance (a fun fact is that the infamous duo Bonnie and Clyde was a Libra-Aries couple). Indeed, this relationship personifies the saying *opposites attract*: Libra expresses himself through *we*, whereas Aries expresses himself through *me*. Although both partners will need to accommodate the other's distinct perspective, this couple can form a fierce, unstoppable partnership.

Libra and Taurus

Seductive Taurus and flirtatious Libra are instantly attracted to each other. Both governed by sensual Venus, these signs are *obsessed* with romance. However, the celestial bull has a distinctive relationship with love. Taurus requires tangible expressions of affection (such as long-stemmed roses and five-course dinners). Libra, on the other hand, is much more cerebral. For the scales, beauty is embedded in sophistication, connoisseurship, and impeccable social finesse. Although they will need to negotiate these differences, Libra's calm diplomacy offsets Taurus's stubborn sensibility, and Taurus's domestic passions complement Libra's aestheticism. Ultimately, Libra and Taurus make a fabulous pair.

Libra and Gemini

When these two similar air signs connect, it's a true meeting of the minds. Both chatty Gemini and elegant Libra love to be intellectually entertained, so the Libra-Gemini duo will enjoy exploring mutual hobbies and interests together—especially those centered around fun social engagements. Gemini will also be inspired by Libra's refined palate, while Libra will be charmed by Gemini's dynamic energy. But be aware that although Libra and Gemini make a terrific pair, each partner will need to ensure that they're prioritizing the relationship. Both Libra and Gemini want to be liked by their peers, which—if not properly communicated—could lead to wandering eyes. For them to build a partnership based on trust and loyalty, they must carve out time to be together *without* the need for external validation. After all, this duo is dynamic enough to generate their own amusement.

Libra and Cancer

The Libra-Cancer relationship isn't always easy to navigate. Cancer (the celestial crab) is extremely self-protective, while Libra (the scales) is much more socially inclined. On a bad day, people-pleasing Libra can become overly consumed by his public image, which will *definitely* rub Cancer the wrong way. Cancer craves safety and security, so Libra's quest to please others can leave her feeling a bit threatened about her own importance in his life. But the conflict isn't one-sided: to amiable Libra, Cancer's armored intensity feels harsh and unwelcoming. However, this relationship can be extremely rewarding: Cancer can teach Libra how to focus his gaze, and Libra can coax Cancer out of her hard shell. When coupled with Cancer, Libra must prove his dedication by paying extra attention to his partner (especially in group settings). Cancer, on the other hand, must learn to trust Libra, which may require her to crawl out of her comfort zone. If these two can find mutual understanding, the Libra-Cancer match will facilitate incredible growth.

When Stars Align

Libra and Cancer can seriously butt heads—but in truth, this is only because they're quite similar. They're both cardinal signs, which means they are great at accomplishing their goals. To strengthen their bond, the Cancer-Libra couple should take time to discuss what they want to achieve—both individually and together. When these cardinal energies align, anything is possible.

Libra and Leo

This pairing works exceptionally well, primarily because Libra and Leo make great friends. Elegant Libra treats Leo like royalty, and regal Leo adores Libra's effortless social finesse. The Libra-Leo couple loves to attend parties, and they encourage each other to embrace their performative spirits. They both love to entertain. However, the celestial lion is not interested in egalitarianism: he expects his partner to worship him—unconditionally—above *anyone* else. Since Libra plays the role of the cosmic diplomat, this air sign may grow to resent Leo's rigid monarchy. Luckily, there's no need for a rebellion: tension between Libra and Leo can be alleviated through honest communication. When these two build their own kingdom together based on trust and loyalty, the Libra-Leo bond has the potential to go from fabulous to forever.

Libra and Virgo

Think of the Libra-Virgo bond as an assembly line: Virgo's role is to analyze a situation, while Libra's is to then balance it. These roles go hand in hand, and since Libra and Virgo sit next to each other in the zodiac wheel, they know how to work together. They bounce information off of each other, each leaning into the other's unique skill set. On a good day, Libra is inspired by Virgo's meticulous eye, and Virgo is enamored by Libra's refined palate. On a bad day, however, they have a difficult time accomplishing their individual goals. Virgo's fussiness makes Libra nervous, while Libra's cavalier attitude makes Virgo feel neglected. Needless to say, all relationships require hard work. Fortunately, when Libra and Virgo invest in their relationship, treating it like a well-oiled machine, it can be exceptionally productive.

Libra and Libra

When Libras link up, they meet in happy harmony. Libra loves to be in relationships, so this match feels almost effortless. In fact, a Libra-Libra bond can escalate quickly, going from zero to one hundred faster than you can say, "I do." But before these air signs exchange vows, they need to make sure they're investing in a union that's built to last. As the peer-mediator of the zodiac, Libra tries to avoid conflict by any means necessary. While this may sound ideal, it can actually be a recipe for disaster. In practice, this ambivalence fosters passive-aggressive behavior, bottled-up resentment, and lots of hurt feelings. Accordingly, these two must learn to communicate their honest experiences through equal parts sharing and listening. If the Libra duo can learn to lead with sincerity, this will be an easy alignment.

Libra and Scorpio

Whoa, did it just get hot in here? Between Scorpio's attraction to Libra's aesthetic and Libra's draw to Scorpio's mystique, there is an instant chemistry between these signs. To put it bluntly, Libra and Scorpio will have *great* sex. But past the seriously steamy sex-capades, a long-term partnership between Libra and Scorpio will require a bit more nuance. Scorpio's intensity scares Libra, who prefers to keep all social dynamics light and easy. Additionally, Scorpio feels slighted by Libra's signature indecisiveness. If this couple can successfully balance their cerebral desires with their physical passions, the Libra-Scorpio pairing can be an incredible force to be reckoned with.

Libra and Sagittarius

Here's the deal: Libra is all about partnership...*in theory*. In reality, this intellectual air sign is more interested in the concept of equity than the actual relationship itself. Interestingly, Sagittarius also prefers the idea of a bond over the real thing: this independent fire sign hates to be stifled by any sort of obligation. Although the Libra-Sagittarius match isn't always perfect (Libra hates conflict, while Sagittarius loves stirring the pot), the combined energy of these signs is infectious. Libra is delighted to join Sagittarius on his adventures, and Sagittarius fuels Libra's curiosity through a shared interest in art and culture. When these two come together, their bond is easy, natural, and—perhaps most importantly—exceptionally playful.

When Stars Align

Libra is diplomatic, so although he is committed to honoring his values, he wants to deliver the information with tact. Sagittarius, on the other hand, *hates* niceties—in fact, he often says controversial things just to watch people squirm. When bonded, they need to make sure they're on the same page; otherwise, sharp-tongued Sagittarius could turn Libra's elegant cocktail party into a total disaster.

Libra and Capricorn

At first, stoic Capricorn admires Libra's appreciation for balance and encourages him to continue cultivating his distinctive moral code. Libra will also bend to suit Capricorn's needs—but this air sign still wants to have fun. In Libra's world, social harmony is more important than righteousness. Subsequently, the Libra-Capricorn match may become compromised when Capricorn grows suspicious of Libra's flirtatious nature, and Libra begins to find Capricorn's focus on pragmatism overly serious and conservative. In order to make this match work, both Libra and Capricorn will need to find mutual respect for the other's core differences and concede enough to strike a balanced partnership. When they do commit, they can create a lasting bond.

Libra and Aquarius

Both air signs, Libra and Aquarius care deeply about social issues. Libra, of course, wants to be well liked, whereas Aquarius's interests are more politically oriented. At first, Aquarius's desire to rebel against the establishment may scare diplomatic Libra, but gradually Libra will learn to embrace Aquarius's effortless cool. And once Aquarius learns to accept Libra's people-pleasing nature, he will enjoy the freedom that goes along with dating a social butterfly (both Libra and Aquarius are comfortable doing their own thing). When the Libra-Aquarius couple aligns on their shared values and interests, this relationship is spirited, intellectual, and exceptionally dynamic.

> **When Stars Align**
> Libra and Aquarius have very different ways of moving through the world: Libra is all about unity, while Aquarius is all about independence. When push comes to shove, however, this combined air energy can generate some serious wind power (Libra John Lennon and Aquarius Yoko Ono are a perfect example).

Libra and Pisces

Both pacifists, Libra and Pisces enter a relationship together through their mutual appreciation for creativity and kindness. Inspired by the arts (especially music), they enjoy filling their weekends with concerts, museum trips, and dynamic workshops. However, Pisces is the last sign of the zodiac, so this water sign has a deep wisdom that sometimes manifests as intense sadness. These dark waters can disturb Libra, who, as an air sign, always tries to maintain a cheerful disposition. However, this pairing will offer each sign something worth fighting for: Libra will teach Pisces how to lighten up, while Pisces will help Libra dig below his surface interests. If Libra can learn to lead with empathy instead of judgment, and Pisces can let Libra's air energy calm her waves, the Libra-Pisces bond will surely be successful.

Love Planets: Venus and Mars

Your Sun sign helps you understand your essence (the wants, needs, and special things that make you, well, *you*), which is extremely important in exploring romantic compatibility. However, this sign is just one component of your rich, complex astrological profile. The birth chart (a snapshot of the sky at your exact moment of birth) features a number of planets—each with its own functions and purposes. Of these, Venus and Mars reveal critical information about your romantic sensibilities. In astrology, Venus is linked to love, beauty, and money. You can look to Venus to understand the way you idealize partnership and approach relationships. Mars governs ambition, momentum, and sex. When exploring romantic compatibility, it's important to also look at the role of Mars within your astrological profile, as its placement will reveal insight into your preferences...between the sheets.

And, let's be honest, whether a relationship lasts for one night or a lifetime, sexual attraction is a major part of the equation.

Venus in Libra

Venus governs Libra, so this romantic planet loves to work with Libra's energy. Since Libra is obsessed with balance, harmony, and symmetry, Venus in Libra is a total aesthete. He loves to indulge his exquisite style and sophisticated taste within his partnerships. Simply put, Venus in Libra needs to be in a relationship that doesn't just align in practice, but also looks good on paper.

Mars in Libra

Sure, Libra is fair—but this peaceful sign is anything but decisive (as the celestial scales, Libra can become obsessed with weighing the pros and cons). When aggressive Mars comes into the picture, Libra has a particularly difficult time committing to a choice. Although Mars in Libra finds inspiration everywhere (he is exceptionally creative), he prefers taking direction to giving orders. In terms of sexuality, however, his indecision isn't a bad thing: Mars in Libra is very curious and has quite the appetite for adventure.

Chapter 8

Scorpio

(October 23–November 21)

Scorpio has a bit of a reputation. This mysterious water sign is renowned for her spellbinding allure, relentless ambition, and signature elusiveness (which also makes her the most enigmatic sign of the zodiac). Scorpio is also represented by the scorpion, the infamous arachnid that dwells in the shadows, only revealing itself when prompted to pounce. Likewise for Scorpio, life is a chess game, but with her meticulous maneuvers, this mystical sign can always guarantee a "checkmate."

Power from Below

Scorpio is ruled by the planet Pluto. In roman mythology, Pluto (and his Greek counterpart, Hades) is the god of the underworld: the judge of the dead, and the ruler of wealth. Though the term *underworld* often evokes images of Dante's fiery *Inferno*, in astrology this realm is not nearly as sinister. In fact, both freedom (that is, the ability to slip off the shackles of judgment and celebrate your most authentic self) and fortune (in the form of subterranean resources, like diamonds and oil) exist here.

Written in the Stars

One could talk about Scorpio's dark and mysterious qualities all day—but keep in mind that there's more to this water sign than just doom and gloom. Scorpio also loves to have fun! Whether she is dancing at a nightclub, sipping coffee with friends, or watching a favorite movie, she definitely enjoys a good time.

Within the underworld, you are empowered by your ability to regenerate and become the best, strongest version of yourself. Scorpio is associated with the main regenerative themes of death, sex, and transformation. Evolution is essential for Scorpio, who uses metamorphosis (moving between different types of philosophies, aesthetics, and artistic passions) as a tool for emotional and psychic expansion. Just like Pluto and the seductive powers of the underworld, Scorpio oozes a bewitching magnetism. Indeed, she has *no* problem attracting lovers. In fact, this celestial arachnid is known for her incredible eroticism. Despite her lusty reputation, however, she values loyalty and intimacy in all relationships.

Emotional Depth

Due to her incredible passion and power, Scorpio is often mistaken for a fire sign. However, she is actually a water sign, which means she derives her strength from the subconscious, emotional realm. Like her fellow water signs (Cancer and Pisces), Scorpio is extremely intuitive and sensitive. She can pick up on the energy in any room and absorb the emotions of others.

> **Written in the Stars**
> Scorpio is associated with all that exists under the surface: she is like the roots beneath the tree. Fittingly, she has an incredible green thumb. Whether she is gardening in her backyard or tending to an indoor plant, Scorpio can effortlessly infuse magic into the soil. It's an amazing gift!

But what makes this sign so distinctive is her venomous sting. Unlike Cancer, who exists within a protective shell, Scorpio's skin is also her armor: this arachnid is tough through and through. And just like her astrological symbol, Scorpio lurks in the shadows, waiting for the perfect opportunity to strike when least expected. This calculating water sign is constantly plotting several steps ahead: everything is part of a bigger scheme. But her intentions aren't necessarily nefarious; she simply knows what she wants from the start, and she enjoys playing the long game in order to get it. She is extremely focused on her goals, and she'll *never* show her cards—and it is this enigmatic nature that makes her so seductive and beguiling.

The Shadow Realm: Scorpio Quirks

On a good day, Pluto's influence drives Scorpio to be ambitious; she uses her incredible internal power to move mountains and is always willing to root for the underdog. She identifies with the archetype of the dark horse that unexpectedly wins the race. After all, the celestial scorpion moves in the shadows: she *prefers* when no one sees her rise to the top. On a bad day, however, Scorpio's own shadowy side takes over, and she becomes driven by a relentless desire for control. This need stems in part from her being a fixed sign (born at the height of the fall season), a quality that bestows upon her a stubbornness that is matched by few. In these instances, Scorpio may use her incredible intuition to manipulate situations and pit people against each other. She must remember that if she allows herself to be controlled by her desire for power, she risks stinging herself. Her sneaky behavior may cost her genuine relationships. After all, no one wants to feel like a pawn in someone's personal game of chess.

Ultimately, this sign is at her best when this intrinsic intensity is applied to soulful connections with her closest companions. The truth is, though she can be overly jealous and possessive, she is also extremely protective of her loved ones, ready to stand up for them without a second thought. When she builds trust with others and leads with confidence, Scorpio demonstrates unparalleled empathy, depth, and commitment. By focusing on empowerment versus control, she can use her skills to help both herself and her loved ones grow.

Written in the Stars

Scorpio is an extremely sensitive creature. It's not easy for her to open up and talk about her feelings, but trust that your Scorpio partner has an extremely deep connection to the people and things that surround her. In fact, Scorpio is quite nostalgic. Don't be surprised if she has a memory box (or two) filled with mementos from the past.

Casting a Spell: Attracting Scorpio

Scorpio is usually pretty informal. Although she can dress up at a moment's notice, she prefers to be comfortable. However, she will be impressed by the sight of someone enchantingly stylish (keep in mind she prefers tasteful and elegant looks, not those that are overly ostentatious). Further, she is always seduced by scent. As a sensitive water sign, the celestial scorpion has very acute senses, so when it comes to romance, it's wise to indulge these points of passion. She is particularly attracted to pungent, organic aromas. Musk, frankincense, myrrh, and ambergris are great options, as they are distinctive and also a little mysterious. A dash of one of these scents (as perfume, cologne, or home fragrance) will definitely intrigue your Scorpio lover and keep her coming back for more.

It's also no surprise that Halloween occurs during Scorpio season: this shadow-dwelling water sign is totally enchanted by everything mysterious and supernatural. This includes ghost stories, so when wooing Scorpio, be sure to share your favorite paranormal experiences!

Passing the Tests

This intense, shadow-residing water sign values her privacy, so it's not easy for her to let a new partner into her heart (this is why she often goes back to an ex). Needless to say, if you're interested in pursuing Scorpio, expect a long courtship process riddled with *lots* of tests of your emotional strength. And since every move she makes is intentional, you'll have to be quick to keep up with her. For this mysterious sign, *everything* is a symbol, embedded with layers upon layers of meaning—so no, that smiley face at the end of her last text message was definitely not innocent.

If you can successfully get through Scorpio's examination process, she will finally be ready to develop a soul connection. But unlike the zodiac's other more guarded signs (such as Cancer and Virgo), partnership doesn't ease Scorpio: her intensity continues in the partnership, as her main focus becomes locking in her partner—for life.

Mysterious Seduction

In medical astrology, Scorpio governs the groin and reproductive organs. Indeed, there truly is no zodiac sign more closely connected to sex than Scorpio is. This water sign is known for her hypnotic seduction style and insatiable appetite. Though misconceptions plague many astrological signs (Gemini is seen as two-faced; Virgo as prudish), this is one instance in which the rumors are true: Scorpio is *extremely* sexual.

Written in the Stars

Is your Scorpio partner's birthday between October 23 and November 9? If so, she was born when the sun was "Via Combusta." Ancient astrologers believed that under this sky, the sun was moving through a "fiery road." Although most modern astrologers don't incorporate this into their practices, one thing is for sure: this Scorpio lover is *especially* passionate!

Her sensuality combines raw passion with the soulful intensity of water energy. Intimacy with Scorpio is an experience for the mind, body, *and* spirit. She also isn't afraid to explore power play and is aroused by themes of dominance and submission. Specifically, Scorpio should experiment with kinkier activities, including bondage (of course, consent and boundaries must be established first). When she feels physically connected to her partner, she'll be delighted to expand her sexual horizons.

However, despite her proclivities, the physical act of intimacy is often less important for Scorpio than the intensity of the connection. It's not easy for Scorpio to satisfy her appetite, and thus this water sign is often drawn to dark and mysterious experiences. Indeed, Scorpio is fueled by the danger of clandestine romances. Exceptionally private, she will take extra measures to make sure any hidden liaisons never see the light of day.

Embrace the Shadows: Maintaining a Relationship with Scorpio

Since Scorpio can often fixate on power and control, it's easy for her to become obsessive in her relationships. If, for instance, she fears her partner isn't equally invested in the bond, that shadowy side of her personality will come into play. This "shadow self" may take the form of paranoia, where Scorpio *creates* conflict to test her lover's devotion—a toxic behavior that often backfires. Scorpio must remember that even in serious relationships, people are entitled to emotional autonomy and individuality. If she is not careful, her stinger may end up poisoning the bond.

But the shadow self is nothing to fear—in fact, everyone has one, regardless of whether or not their Sun sign is Scorpio. Further, *because* Scorpio is so in touch with her dark side, it's actually quite easy for her to mitigate any negative tendencies. The most important thing to remember when maintaining a relationship with Scorpio is to be transparent. Ask a lot of questions, be up front about your own thoughts and feelings, and don't be afraid to challenge any sneaky behavior. Scorpio will appreciate being held accountable, and the more that you engage her through direct dialogue, the more you'll be able to build an honest and secure bond.

Unfortunately, heartbreak is inevitable in life, and while Scorpio is known for her ability to rise from the ashes, it doesn't mean breakups are easy for her. In fact, this water sign has an extremely difficult time letting go of her partners. It doesn't matter whether or not Scorpio is the one initiating the split: this intense sign *always* feels jilted after a breakup. Simply put, the end of a relationship triggers her signature desire for control, sometimes causing her to obsess over her former partnerships. She wants to control how an ex responds to the breakup, from what they say about her, to when they begin dating again. So, it's best to nip this tendency in the bud early by calling her out on any borderline-stalker behavior. Explain that there's a no-tolerance policy in your relationship when it comes to fixating on old flames. Scorpio will appreciate your honesty and try her hardest to squash these urges. Sure, there may be a few slipups along the way, but, hey, she's only human!

Lessons in Love: What Is Scorpio's Greatest Fear?

Scorpio is terrified of being discovered. She takes her privacy *extremely* seriously, so even if she is not hiding a massive secret, she feels very protective of her inner world. Never, *ever* go through Scorpio's journals, emails, or text messages. Even if you don't find anything scandalous, Scorpio will be sure to end the relationship instantly: she has a zero-tolerance policy for snooping.

Throughout this process, the mysterious Scorpio will maintain a calm and collected facade—after all, she doesn't want anyone to know her secret plans. Instead, she often manifests her emotions through veiled compulsive behavior. For instance, she may block her ex on social media, but then create a secret account to follow their activity without detection. The best way for Scorpio to fix her broken heart is to look within, face her fears, and allow herself to fully process her darker emotions.

Sun Sign Love Matches

Fueled by her emotions, it's no surprise that Scorpio makes an extremely dedicated partner. While some signs balk at Scorpio's intensity (perceiving her elaborate schemes to be sneaky or manipulative), other signs are inspired by her transformative energy. So, who will steal Scorpio's heart? In the following sections, you'll explore how this celestial arachnid operates in a romantic relationship with each of the twelve signs of the zodiac.

Scorpio and Aries

In traditional astrology (that is, before the telescope was invented), Mars ruled both Aries and Scorpio. Through this ruling, Aries was linked to outward expression, while Scorpio symbolized internal power. Although Scorpio is now ruled by Pluto, Mars's energy is still the force behind the Scorpio-Aries bond. These signs have an incredible physical attraction. However, Aries's inability to keep a secret (one of the celestial ram's signature traits, in fact) deeply disturbs mysterious Scorpio, who values privacy above all else. Meanwhile, Aries is baffled by Scorpio's covert nature and wonders why *everything* needs to be so hush-hush. But at the end of the day, if these two can respect each other's needs, the Scorpio-Aries duo may actually take over the world.

Scorpio and Taurus

There is an incredible magnetism between Scorpio and Taurus. As astrological opposites, these two sit across from each other on the zodiac wheel. Taurus corresponds with the spring, so her connection to the world is primarily physical. The celestial bull loves to watch the flowers bloom. As her inverse sign, Scorpio is all about what lies *beneath* the buds: she represents transformation from within (the raw physicality that defines intimacy, including hormones). That's right: Scorpio is pure sex. So, when paired with Taurus (the most sensual sign of the zodiac), Scorpio's fierce sexual appetite is finally satiated. Although these two will have obstacles to overcome (both are incredibly stubborn), the Scorpio-Taurus couple makes for a truly erotic pairing.

When Stars Align

When Scorpio and Taurus connect, they meet in the middle of an entire life cycle: Taurus symbolizes birth, while Scorpio symbolizes completion. Though these two cosmic bookends are usually well matched, they will need to find ways to compromise when a situation calls for it. Not everything in life has to be so extreme!

Scorpio and Gemini

Scorpio and Gemini make for an eccentric pair. There will definitely be some major obstacles within this bond—Scorpio's core values couldn't be more different from

Gemini's mercurial sensibilities. Gemini is chatty and sociable, and *loves* to change his mind. Scorpio, on the other hand, is intense, private, and steadfast in her convictions. Usually, Scorpio's powerful stinger can seduce even the largest creatures, but the celestial arachnid is no match for the twin: Gemini makes Scorpio's head spin. In order for the Scorpio-Gemini match to last long term, each sign will need to accept the other's differences. If Scorpio can release her urge to micromanage, and Gemini is willing to let Scorpio win *once in a while*, the Scorpio-Gemini bond can be extremely enchanting.

When Stars Align

As water signs, Scorpio and Cancer have a lot in common, but there are definitely key differences between these creatures. For one, Cancer is possessive, while Scorpio is obsessive. Ultimately, they should work together to help mitigate these tendencies.

Scorpio and Cancer

Both water signs, the Scorpio-Cancer relationship flows effortlessly. While some signs balk at Scorpio's intensity, Cancer embraces these emotions. In fact, the celestial crab comes out of her shell for Scorpio: where Cancer is usually guarded at the start of a relationship, with Scorpio she is actually quite vulnerable from the beginning. But even in this magical bond, Scorpio has a difficult time opening up herself. Alas, she is not a crustacean: unlike the crab, the sensitive scorpion cannot abandon her tough exterior. Cancer may get frustrated at times by Scorpio's inability to let go, but at the end of the day, this is one of the best partnerships in the zodiac. When these two commit to each other, they will be sure to mate for life.

Scorpio and Leo

Will Scorpio's venomous sting take down the zodiac's wildcat? Or will the celestial scorpion be squashed by Leo's gigantic paw? When it comes to Scorpio and Leo, the energy is always that of two natural opponents stepping into the ring. Leo and Scorpio are the most jealous signs in the zodiac—so a Scorpio-Leo bond is often fueled by raw intensity. Proud Leo *hates* being left out, and he perceives Scorpio's sneaky movements to be intentionally duplicitous. On the other hand, Scorpio scoffs at Leo's inability to conceal his motives, and she turns up her nose at his performative nature. However, if Scorpio and Leo form a bond, their combined energy is unstoppable. Although it won't be easy, the Scorpio-Leo unit is brave and passionate (both in and out of the bedroom).

Scorpio and Virgo

In a Scorpio-Virgo partnership, both signs love to play up their archetypes: Scorpio wants to seduce, and Virgo wants to *be* seduced. Thus, there is a sexy tension between these two—a push and pull that can form a flirtatious (and kinky) bond. But this connection is more than just leather and lace: the Scorpio-Virgo relationship is built on genuine admiration. Virgo is inspired by Scorpio's ambition, and Scorpio values Virgo's grounded practicality. The occasional conflict will occur when Scorpio feels judged by Virgo and Virgo feels overpowered by Scorpio, but overall, this is a structurally sound match. When both partners are invested, the Scorpio-Virgo relationship is built to last.

Scorpio and Libra

There is an interesting power struggle in the Scorpio-Libra relationship. Scorpio tries to focus Libra's gaze: she wants to be the center of his world. And although Libra likes to feign innocence, the celestial scales enjoys teasing Scorpio with carefree flirtation. When these two autumn signs stop playing games, however, they can actually form a fabulous pair: the ultimate "good cop" (Libra) and "bad cop" (Scorpio) team. Of course, there will be flare-ups (air and water energy together create hurricanes), but friction isn't always a deal breaker. In the case of Scorpio and Libra, it can actually build heat.

Scorpio and Scorpio

It's easy to be amused by the Scorpio-Scorpio bond: these two are constantly trying to freak each other out! Symbolized by the scorpion, Scorpio is proud to be the creepy-crawler of the zodiac. So, when she matches up with one of her own, she works hard to maintain her mysterious intensity. The Scorpio-Scorpio partnership is fueled by secrets, passion, and a need for control, which can make it hard for these two to sustain a long-term relationship. However, if they can make it past the initial scuffles, they will enjoy the companionship. In this dynamic, Scorpio won't need to explain herself: her needs are respected, understood, and—perhaps most importantly—mutual.

When Stars Align

Have you ever watched two Scorpios battle? It's not a pretty sight. When these arachnids link up, they need to be *very* careful not to get nasty with each other: since they share an anatomy, they know just where to point their stingers so it hurts.

Scorpio and Sagittarius

Scorpio is intrigued by Sagittarius, wondering, "Who *is* this fiery archer?" And once she discovers that he is always wandering, her primary mission will be to seduce him into commitment (Scorpio loves a challenge!). Shockingly, however, Scorpio is no match for Sagittarius: even when under the celestial scorpion's spell, the archer needs to roam. Eventually, both Scorpio and Sagittarius may get bored of the bond. After all, Scorpio needs loyalty and a bit of mystery, and Sagittarius needs freedom and honesty. If these two decide to make it work, however, they'll form an interesting relationship defined by lots of push and pull. Hey, no one ever said love was easy!

When Stars Align

Saddle up, Scorpio! Sure, Scorpio loves to control everything—but that's why, every now and then, it's thrilling to just go along for the ride. If Scorpio is willing to sit in the passenger's seat for a change, a Scorpio-Sagittarius partnership can be a truly exhilarating experience.

Scorpio and Capricorn

While most signs can't handle Capricorn's relentless ambition—brushing off the sea goat as a workaholic—Scorpio is inspired by her hustle. In fact, Scorpio will try to woo Capricorn by showcasing her own determination. And she's right to do so: when it comes to long-term partnership, Capricorn is *extremely* particular. Both signs will spend the majority of their courtship inspecting each other's resume, until they eventually develop a romantic—and extremely sexual—bond. Yes, when they've finally finished flaunting their success, Scorpio and Capricorn will direct their gazes toward the bedroom. Here, these enterprising signs *really* get to work. This bond is intense, with both Scorpio and Capricorn expecting long-term commitment.

Scorpio and Aquarius

In the zodiac, signs of the same modality (aka cardinal, fixed, or mutable) form a sharp 90-degree angle known as a square. Although squares are often considered the most difficult aspect to pair together, they also fuel forward motion. And in the case of Scorpio and Aquarius, the tension may be worthwhile. Scorpio and Aquarius are both riddles: everyone is always trying to figure out these signs. Likewise, Scorpio and Aquarius are intrigued by each other and enjoy peeling back the layers of the other's complexity. At the end of the day, power-hungry Scorpio will need to decide whether she can accept Aquarius's independence, and Aquarius, in turn, will need to reconcile Scorpio's issues with control. However, if this square can find a way to make it work, their bond will be magical, mysterious, and teeming with tons of inside jokes. Indeed, the expression for the Scorpio-Aquarius match is *us against the world.*

Scorpio and Pisces

Scorpio is so intense that many people forget she is a water sign rather than a fire sign. However, at the end of the day, the celestial arachnid is fueled by emotion—and there's no sign more invested in feelings than Pisces. Unlike Scorpio, who can navigate both land (the physical) and sea (the subconscious), Pisces is totally immersed in water. Pisces's incredible psychic powers can overwhelm Scorpio, who focuses primarily on a balance between the two realms. However, Pisces's empathy soothes Scorpio, and together these partners will enjoy deep-sea diving into each other's inner worlds. As long as Scorpio stays gentle and Pisces learns to self-advocate, they will love building a majestic kingdom together beneath the waves.

Love Planets: Venus and Mars

Though your Sun sign helps you understand the desires, needs, and little quirks that make up your essence, it is just one component of your complex astrological profile. The birth chart (a snapshot of the sky at your exact moment of birth) also features the planets Venus and Mars, which reveal critical information about your romantic sensibilities. In astrology, Venus is linked to love, beauty, and money. By understanding Venus's function in your astrological profile, you can unlock a deeper understanding of how you idealize partnership and approach your relationships. Mars, meanwhile, governs ambition, momentum, and sex.

When exploring romantic compatibility, it's important to note the placement of this planet in your chart, as it will reveal insight into how you like to "get down." And honestly, whether a relationship lasts one night or an entire lifetime, sexual attraction is a key part of the equation.

Venus in Scorpio

The scorpion is a shadow dweller. Likewise, celestial Scorpio derives her dynamic power from the subconscious realm. Under Scorpio, the sensual planet Venus is no longer interested in a romantic dinner. Venus in Scorpio wants dark, mysterious sex with taboo partners. She loves anything with a dash of danger. Indeed, Venus in Scorpio paints an elusive sky fueled by deep, erotic connection that illuminates from the inside. However, Venus in Scorpio is also seeking deep emotional intimacy. She wants someone who understands her soul, who she can safely open up and reveal her vulnerabilities to.

Mars in Scorpio

Usually, Mars likes to display its strength and determination in the public sector (think gladiators). When Mars is in mysterious Scorpio, however, it derives power from what is under the surface. Mars in Scorpio is all about hidden ambition, so don't be surprised if she emerges as an "overnight success." In reality, she been hustling quietly in the shadows. When it comes to sex, intimacy with Mars in Scorpio is always intense, and seduction (for example, deep conversations at a steamy bar, followed by a quick trip to the establishment's bathroom for some heavy petting) is an *essential* ingredient.

Chapter 9

Sagittarius

(November 22–December 21)

Represented by the archer, Sagittarius is on the eternal quest for knowledge. And as the last fire sign of the zodiac, his journey is guided by his blazing arrows, so he is constantly chasing geographical, intellectual, and metaphysical curiosities. He can be found traversing all corners of the world on his thrill-seeking expeditions. So, when it comes to romance, every day is an adventure with this spirited flamethrower.

Expansion

It's no surprise that Jupiter—the lucky planet of abundance—governs Sagittarius: fortune follows this magical sign everywhere he goes (he seems to be a magnet for unexpected job opportunities, apartment deals, and even lucky lottery tickets!). As the astrological archer, Sagittarius desires mental, philosophical, and spiritual expansion—and a lot of fun along the way. Whether racing up Mount Kilimanjaro, enrolling in yet another academic program, or belting into a microphone at karaoke night, he pushes forward with courage, enthusiasm, and a positive spirit.

Written in the Stars

Sagittarius may be a fearless wanderer, but that doesn't mean he doesn't require some stability. Although he won't often admit it, he depends on personal markers to provide direction. And, more often than not, those checkpoints come in the form of his relationships. That's right: even the most independent Sagittarius needs structure!

In fact, Sagittarius has the incredible ability to transform anything—even the most mundane activity—into a riveting epic. Virtually *everything* in the world has a story, and since Sagittarius is an excellent orator, he can share these tales with friends, family members, and strangers alike in ways that light up the room and spark infectious laughter in his audience. And because this fire sign is effortlessly magnetic, he is *always* surrounded by avid listeners (aka fans). Simply put, this sign is definitely the "popular kid" of the zodiac. He makes friends everywhere he goes, so—whether he likes it or not—Sagittarius is *always* rolling up with an entourage.

As a mutable sign, Sagittarius is also extremely adaptable. Mutable signs occur at the transition of seasons (Gemini, Virgo, Sagittarius, and Pisces correspond with the final weeks of spring, summer, fall, and winter respectively) and, likewise, are associated with change. Indeed, Sagittarius has a deep-rooted desire for frequent change. Sagittarius loves to adopt new philosophies, switch perspectives, and—perhaps most importantly—travel to unchartered places. The explorer of the zodiac, Sagittarius has a nomadic quality. In fact, he may get antsy if he stays in one place for too long. It's also critical that the archer has the freedom to roam (in medical astrology, Sagittarius rules the thighs, which help him stay on the move). Not everyone can keep up with Sagittarius's ever-changing curiosities, so when it comes to romance, this fire sign is definitely known to break hearts.

Thank You and Good Night!: Sagittarius Quirks

Sagittarius is the comedian of the zodiac (along with Virgo, who excels in observational humor). This fire sign is always telling a story, so every conversation is infused with humor, quick wit...and notable bluntness (it's no wonder that Ben Stiller, Sarah Silverman, Richard Pryor, and

Rodney Dangerfield were all born under this hilarious Sun sign!). Indeed, Sagittarius moves through life with a no-BS philosophy that resonates in very matter-of-fact (and quite humorous) comments. However, while his *bon mots* are certainly unrivaled, Sagittarius must remember to be careful with his sharp tongue and biting remarks. Sure, he knows a lot, but he doesn't know *everything*. On occasion, his fiery energy goes a bit overboard, causing him to come off as pretentious or even mean-spirited.

Sagittarius's mutable quality can also make him a bit flakey when it comes to decisions (especially the important ones, like whether to commit to a relationship). With so many possibilities, and pros and cons to each one, he may agonize over which is the "right" partnership or avoid setting anything in stone at all for the sake of keeping his options open. Further, it can sometimes be hard to get a word in edgewise when hanging out with this vivacious storyteller. He doesn't mean to talk over you—he just has so many exciting adventures to share, and limited time to share them, before he gets that itch to jet off on a new one. To avoid feeling overshadowed, be honest with Sagittarius: tell him that you want to get a chance to talk, and be firm. He will surely appreciate the honesty and work to give you more opportunities to speak.

The Romantic Rodeo: Attracting Sagittarius

Have you ever been lost in the Sahara Desert with a limited water supply? Stranded at sea? Caught in an avalanche?

Sagittarius has! With his unyielding adventurous spirit, dating Sagittarius is like sitting in the passenger seat of a Jeep Wrangler off-roading on rough terrain: exciting, bumpy, and extremely unpredictable. After all, he likes to live on the edge, where there is a greater chance of discovering something new. Yes, *danger* is his middle name, so when it comes to romance, he may be tempted to pursue a high-stakes partnership (for example, trying to woo his boss).

Lessons in Love: Where Should You Take Sagittarius for a Date?

Sagittarius is a philosopher and among the most intellectually curious signs of the zodiac, which mean he's always testing out new theories. Make exploration the theme of a date: whether you check out a foreign film, hike a mysterious trail, or attend a lecture on an esoteric subject, this fiery archer will love diving into a new fascination!

It's not easy to get Sagittarius's attention. After all, the archer doesn't often stay in one place long enough to sustain interest. Accordingly, if you're trying to court Sagittarius, you'll need to keep this dynamic sign on his toes. Don't be afraid to be loud, and showcase the most spirited aspects of your personality. If Sagittarius isn't listening, grab a knife and click your glass. Yell into a megaphone. Stomp on the ground. Do whatever it takes to make sure he knows it's your turn to speak. It may seem abrasive at first, but trust that Sagittarius will be drawn to your self-advocacy. Also, be sure to keep your communication style varied, switching between phone calls, texting, and in-person conversations. And when you do confirm a date, keep plenty of room for spontaneity: leave an hour after dinner to explore a trail near the restaurant, or slip in a surprise stop for the latest dessert craze.

Sexual Adventures

Playful and free-spirited, the archer tends to have a carefree attitude when it comes to sex: his physical relationships can vary from casual to committed. And since he is a natural explorer, sex is *always* an adventure for this fiery sign. More specifically, Sagittarius views physical intimacy as an opportunity for self-discovery and intellectual expansion—so when it comes to getting down, he tends to be a serious thrill-seeker. Brainstorm new, exciting ways of dialing up your sexual encounters with Sagittarius. Don't be afraid to get into taboos like making out in an alley or in a bar's bathroom. It may seem risky...but that's just the way Sagittarius likes it. Sex in unexpected places is another *huge* turn-on for this stallion, so move the intimacy outdoors the next time you want to get frisky. Sagittarius's erogenous zones are the hips and thighs, so saddle up in reverse cowgirl–type positions! You can guarantee a wild ride with this erotic equestrian.

Lessons in Love: What's the Difference Between Love and Lust?

With the fiery archer, it's not always easy to tell the difference between true love and a star-crossed booty call. In fact, at the beginning there's really no difference between the two: passionate Sagittarius is often driven by infatuation. Over time, however, it will be easier to tell whether he is sticking around, because, well, he is sticking around. If you're still having a difficult time qualifying Sagittarius's feelings, just ask: he is extremely straightforward and will appreciate your candor.

Choosing a Copilot: Maintaining a Relationship with Sagittarius

Sagittarius energy is that of a wildfire: blazing, expansive, and sometimes dangerous. Likewise, this adrenaline junky is known to be fiercely independent. But, when Sagittarius does decide to couple up...well, nothing really changes. While cruising down the Amazon River with your mate is fabulous, most people can't maintain a daredevil lifestyle 24/7. So, if Sagittarius always prioritizes excitement over commitment, his adventures in life are likely to remain solo. Serious relationships are about sharing your vulnerabilities, creating a practical support system, and tackling daily realities together (yes, even when they're mundane).

If your schedule can't support Sagittarius's proposed itinerary, you can still try making every day an adventure. Start a daily ritual of doing a crossword puzzle together, or try *Wikipedia* roulette (randomly selecting a page and sharing the results with each other). Sagittarius loves collecting knowledge, so he'll be sure to appreciate these cerebral activities. Ultimately, some of the most exciting explorations are those that fuel emotional growth. The journey within will always be rewarding. Consider exploring an alternative wellness practice with your Sagittarius partner, for instance. Whether it involves astrology, Reiki, or yoga, Sagittarius will love expanding his spiritual horizons with you by his side.

When it comes down to it, Sagittarius is simply seeking a copilot. He wants to be with someone fun and adventurous, who challenges him to broaden his horizons. Even within a committed relationship, Sagittarius resents boundaries, so if you find yourself involved with this sign, be sure to have your passport ready. You won't know what's coming, but it's bound to be a wild ride.

However, some boundaries aren't necessarily a bad thing—in fact, they can help provide a solid framework for the relationship. When partnered with Sagittarius, try establishing things early on that clarify the dos and don'ts of your partnership. For instance, if you want your Sagittarius mate to send you a good night message before bed, say so from the beginning. It will be easier for Sagittarius to understand the relationship if the parameters are clear.

Dangerous Flames

Since Sagittarius is always seeking new thrills, his freedom needs to be honored in order to sustain any long-term relationship. When he is in need of a solo trip, sit back and enjoy your own alone time. A few texts here and there are nice, but trust that he will fill you in on everything once he returns. Of course, Sagittarius should also keep in mind that adventures can be twice as satisfying with a companion. Let him know that you're ready and eager to participate in his quests, but allow him to make the decision for himself, and avoid guilt-tripping him if he chooses to go it alone.

Written in the Stars

Want to irritate Sagittarius? Tell him no. Sagittarius *hates* being told what to do—especially if he perceives it as stifling his freedom. In fact, the fastest way to get the archer to run away is to tell him to stay.

Sagittarius is very blunt, so when he does initiate a breakup, the terms are quite straightforward. When Sagittarius says it's over, it is truly *over*. There will be no wavering, no late-night text messages, and *definitely* no heartfelt apology voicemails. A nomad at heart, he finds it easy to pack up and leave when things aren't working out. In fact, Sagittarius can often move forward as if a relationship never even existed in the first place. While this may seem harsh, remember that wildfire simply isn't meant to be contained.

Sun Sign Love Matches

Sagittarius's energy is *definitely* distinctive. While certain zodiac signs are inspired by his high-octane lifestyle, others may have a difficult time reconciling his unpredictability. So, will you surf his fiery blaze...or get scorched by the flames? Grab a lasso, partner: in the following sections, you'll find out just how each sign can wrangle this sexy stallion.

Sagittarius and Aries

The last fire sign of the zodiac, Sagittarius's energy is infectious: he is boundless, brazen, and extremely curious. In fact, most signs can't keep up with his flames. Aries, however, is inspired by this active sign. Aries's own youthful energy perfectly complements Sagittarius's wildfire, and within the bond, both partners are motivated to explore their innate curiosities. But they need to be careful! Although the Sagittarius-Aries bond can last a lifetime, this couple is definitely combustible, as both signs can be extremely volatile. Each partner should be sure to give the other plenty of space to sizzle after a dispute.

Sagittarius and Taurus

Sagittarius and Taurus have completely different needs and interests. Taurus requires the safety and security of a comfort zone, whereas Sagittarius needs the excitement and spontaneity of exploration. Taurus links success to objects, whereas Sagittarius associates his achievements with adventure. Taurus is proud of her steadfast ideologies, whereas Sagittarius values the ability to change his mind. However, although these two signs exist in totally different universes, they are capable of coming together in a relationship. If they can find a way to appreciate their opposing views, the Sagittarius-Taurus bond offers a powerful counterbalance that inspires *both* signs to try something new.

When Stars Align

If Sagittarius had things his way, he would abandon all earthly possessions, strip naked, and live in the forest contemplating the meaning of life. For Taurus, however, this plan sounds absolutely *horrific*—well, except for the forest part: earthy Taurus does like to be in nature. So, why not meet in the middle? The Sagittarius-Taurus couple can rent a cabin (Taurus, of course, will have the final word on the accommodations) with plenty of acreage so Sagittarius can go exploring...but still be back in time for dinner.

Sagittarius and Gemini

Sagittarius and Gemini are opposite signs, meaning they face each other on the zodiac wheel. Not all opposite signs are compatible, but the Sagittarius-Gemini bond is one of the most dynamic partnerships in astrology. Sagittarius is all about the big picture. Gemini, on the other hand, is motivated by what exists at the microlevel. This air sign focuses on all of the small details, filling in the gaps in Sagittarius's broad strokes. When partnered, these two signs inspire each other in their inquisitiveness.

Sagittarius and Cancer

When it comes to matters of the heart, *anything* is possible. However, there are some cosmic matches that may require a bigger miracle, and the Sagittarius-Cancer relationship is at the very top of that list. When this bond is at its best, Sagittarius loves to share his stories with Cancer, who is a terrific listener. However, these two signs exist in completely different dimensions. Cancer requires domesticity in order to feel secure, while Sagittarius's happiness is dependent on his room to roam. Of course, honest communication is always key, so if Sagittarius and Cancer are brave enough to push forward together, open dialogue will help propel this bond.

Sagittarius and Leo

There is a *ton* of passion in this bond. Sagittarius is charmed by performative Leo, and Leo is totally smitten with fiery Sagittarius. Individually, these signs have two of the biggest personalities of the zodiac, so when they get together, the Sagittarius-Leo dynamic is passionate, creative, and full of life. Simply put, it just makes sense. However, these like-minded fire signs will quickly discover that no relationship is perfect. The proud celestial lion needs the stability and loyalty of a dependable partner, and Sagittarius is often unable to offer that security. It's not personal: no relationship will *ever* supersede Sagittarius's independence. This, of course, is difficult for Leo to reconcile, so the couple can expect conflicts to crop up from time to time. At the end of the day, however, this bond is rewarding for both partners, and when Sagittarius *is* ready to come back home, Leo will surely be waiting.

When Stars Align

Sagittarius can get along with any sign, but he has a special connection to Leo. A fellow fire sign, Leo's regality draws in Sagittarius. Although the archer may give his lion lover a hard time (Sagittarius loves to tease!), there's nothing he enjoys more than pairing up with another flamethrower.

Sagittarius and Virgo

On paper, these two couldn't be a less likely pair: Virgo loves to label and organize, and wildfire Sagittarius hates to feel contained. Since Sagittarius is always chasing his arrow, this archer has a reputation for being a bit unreliable. Logical Virgo will have a difficult time keeping up with his ever-changing itinerary, so when partnered, Sagittarius should be sure to treat his earthy Virgo mate like a copilot. Virgo may not initiate the adventure, but when push comes to shove, she is also a very curious creature. While it's true that there will be some tension in the Sagittarius-Virgo partnership, this couple can find common ground through shared interests and explore the opportunity to create a language that is entirely their own.

Sagittarius and Libra

The Sagittarius-Libra couple often start out as friends. Both of these signs are extremely cerebral, so they connect on an intellectual level. Of course, sexual tension develops quickly: Libra is governed by Venus, while Sagittarius is ruled by Jupiter—the two planets known as auspicious "benefics"—so this union is extremely indulgent. Everything is larger than life with these two signs...including conflict. Sagittarius gets frustrated by Libra's people-pleasing nature, and Libra can become easily annoyed with Sagittarius's blunt attitude. But even at their worst, Sagittarius and Libra truly understand each other. As long as Libra speaks from the heart and Sagittarius keeps his cool, their romantic spark will continue to burn brightly.

Sagittarius and Scorpio

Scorpio is intense and brooding, while Sagittarius is carefree and optimistic. How will these two ever work? The answer exists in their common ground. Although quite different in many ways, both Scorpio and Sagittarius are extremely passionate people. Scorpio's passion is driven by emotion, while Sagittarius's is fueled by curiosity. When bonded, these passions create a dynamic energy focused on living life to the fullest. And the amazing sex helps: these two can't keep their hands off each other! Though long-term success will require compromise, Scorpio and Sagittarius definitely have something special.

Sagittarius and Sagittarius

When archers align their bows, their arrows propel even farther into the distance. A Sagittarius-Sagittarius couple is a terrific pairing: together, they love to travel, learn, and—perhaps most importantly—have fun! Neither takes life too seriously, which, at the end of the day, can make it hard for these two to form a long-lasting, committed partnership. Since neither archer would ever *dare* confine the other, it will take a long time for the Sagittarius-Sagittarius pair to become "official." But, truth be told, that's just the way these archers like it. This pair will always be more committed to their individual curiosities than to coupledom.

Sagittarius and Capricorn

From the start, there's a tension between Sagittarius and Capricorn that is tough to overcome. Sagittarius is governed by Jupiter, while Capricorn is ruled by Saturn—the two planets that are considered "head honchos" in astrology. Jupiter is all about expansion, whereas Saturn is linked to constriction. Likewise, the Sagittarius-Capricorn bond can feel like a contradiction. However, through thoughtful communication and mutual understanding, this match can definitely succeed. Sagittarius may never understand why Capricorn is *so* serious all the time, and Capricorn is baffled by Sagittarius's unyielding positivity, but at the end of the day, their connection is built on respect. When both partners exhibit confidence, and allow each other to do their own thing, this partnership has the potential to last a lifetime.

When Stars Align

Sagittarius and Capricorn should also focus on shared interests in order to ensure long-term success. For instance, both Sagittarius and Capricorn are extremely philosophical: they'll enjoy discussing politics, religion, and science. Although they may have different *perspectives*, establishing common ground is imperative.

Sagittarius and Aquarius

Sagittarius and Aquarius enjoy a remarkable chemistry. Both of these signs are fiercely independent, so each values the other's unique approach to life. Although Sagittarius is more indulgent than humanitarian Aquarius, both signs know that life exists outside of their own immediate reality. Sagittarius and Aquarius also both want to break the rules and challenge the establishment. In fact, individuality and nonconformity are such driving forces behind this partnership that it may be difficult for them to establish an identity as a couple. However, if they are willing to meet in the middle—perhaps by creating a relationship manifesto—this radical pair will be sure to make waves. In fact, Sagittarius and Aquarius may not just inspire *each other*: these two have the potential to change *the world*.

When Stars Align

Both Sagittarius and Aquarius value their freedom, but a key difference between the two is that Sagittarius wants to learn, whereas Aquarius wants to innovate. Accordingly, when it comes to world issues, Sagittarius may be a bit more optimistic than his air sign partner. In order for Aquarius to start a revolution, he must first rebel against something.

Sagittarius and Pisces

There's a powerful attraction between Sagittarius and Pisces. Both of these signs are the largest manifestation of their astrological element: Sagittarius is a wildfire, and Pisces is an ocean. Fortunately, since each sign is so expansive (in fact, in traditional astrology, both Sagittarius *and* Pisces are ruled by larger-than-life Jupiter), neither can ever completely engulf the other. Sagittarius is particularly enchanted by Pisces's vivid imagination, while Pisces is intrigued by Sagittarius's adventurous spirit. Indeed, both Sagittarius and Pisces are wanderers, so it may be hard to anchor this bond in reality. However, if both partners are happy with keeping the relationship in a less defined, more ethereal realm, they will flourish as a truly magical couple.

When Stars Align

When Sagittarius and Pisces align, they need to make sure they don't inadvertently end up sprinting (or in the case of Pisces, swimming) in opposite directions, as both signs are always on the move. When coupled, these adventurous signs should be sure to plan many exciting weekend trips—both on land and in water.

Love Planets: Venus and Mars

Your Sun sign helps you understand your essence (the sum of your desires, needs, and special quirks), which is extremely important in exploring romantic compatibility. However, this sign is just one component of your complex astrological profile. Your birth chart (that is, a snapshot of the sky at your exact moment of birth) features a number of planets—each embedded with its own functions. Of these, Venus and Mars reveal critical information about your romantic sensibilities. In astrology, Venus is linked to love, beauty, and money. Simply put, you can look to

Venus to understand the way you idealize partnership and approach your relationships. Mars, meanwhile, governs ambition, momentum, and sex. The placement of this planet in your chart will reveal important insights into your sexual preferences. And, let's be honest, whether a relationship lasts one night or an entire lifetime, sexual attraction is a key piece of the puzzle.

Venus in Sagittarius

Sagittarius is associated with expansion and exploration. Fittingly, when the planet of love occupies this sign, its focus shifts from romance to rodeos. Venus in Sagittarius is drawn to nonconformists and risk-takers—specifically nomads and daredevils. Adventure is extremely attractive to this fiery partner, though the truth is that *nothing* excites him more than a great sense of humor. Venus in Sagittarius loves to be entertained, so laughter will always be the best medicine...and aphrodisiac.

Mars in Sagittarius

Mars in Sagittarius is motivated by the unknown. Under this sky, Mars's determination is fueled by the passion and excitement quintessential to Sagittarius. Mars in Sagittarius seeks adventure and, with an optimistic spirit, is determined to uncover all that exists at the edges of reality. In fact, he never sticks around in one place for long: he has (faraway) places to be! Fittingly, sex with Mars in Sagittarius is always new and exciting. This lover is especially drawn to outdoor affection, so public make-out sessions will surely delight.

Chapter 10

Capricorn

(December 22–January 19)

Capricorn is represented by the sea goat, an animal with the body of a goat and the tail of a fish. This mysterious creature can navigate both the land and water, symbolizing Capricorn's innate ability to seamlessly engage both her logic and intuition. The most ambitious sign of the zodiac, she certainly knows how to put these skills to use. But don't be fooled: she may appear to be "all work, and no play," but behind the scenes, Capricorn has a wild side.

The World of Saturn

Capricorn is ruled by taskmaster Saturn, the stoic planet that governs time and restrictions. Saturn's role in the zodiac is to teach tough lessons, and—for better or worse—Capricorn is no stranger to growing pains. With this tough planet guiding her experiences, it is likely she was exposed to difficulties at an early age. Because of this, Capricorn is said to age backward. Having already endured hardships in her past, she becomes increasingly youthful, optimistic, and playful as she matures.

Written in the Stars

Capricorn represents the father in astrology, while her opposite sign, Cancer, represents the mother. Additionally, Saturn, Capricorn's planetary ruler, is often referred to in mythology as Father Time. These energies aren't about gender orientation, but rather, how you take care of yourself and others. The moon (Cancer's ruling planet) reflects nurturing, while Saturn reflects handling responsibilities.

This resilience and strength of character also plays into her ambitious nature; Capricorn easily taps into her inner fortitude to overcome whatever stands between her and her long-term goals. Simply put, this sea goat won't let anything—or anyone—get in the way of her success. Capricorn always has a five-year plan and aims to see it through. As a cardinal sign (born at the start of the winter season), Capricorn is especially excellent at taking action, launching initiatives, and assuming leadership positions. Indeed, her can-do attitude leads to success in pretty much any industry (Michelle Obama, Kate Moss, and Elvis Presley are all sea goats).

Letting Loose

After a long day's work, however, Capricorn is delighted to let loose with her closest companions. This earth sign values quality time with her friends and partners, and she enjoys building a community with like-minded over-achievers. Surprisingly, inside every serious Capricorn is a *very* mischievous troublemaker (in tarot, Capricorn is symbolized by the Devil card). Though she seems a bit traditional and conservative at first, Capricorn's confidants know this sea goat can become a *real* party animal. Although she isn't as into massive raves, in smaller, more intimate hangouts she is often the wildest guest, encouraging her friends to stay out past their bedtimes for extra rounds of drinks or late-night karaoke.

Written in the Stars

Capricorn is also quite creative. In fact, some of the most incredible artists, musicians, and actors were born under this sky. Janis Joplin, David Bowie, Jean-Michel Basquiat, and Ava Gardner capture the sea goat spirit, seamlessly fusing ambition and art.

Cold As Ice: Capricorn Quirks

Capricorn's ambition is inspiring; however, because of her unwavering focus, she also has a bit of a reputation for being cold and unemotional. Because she is always thinking about the big picture, she doesn't have the time or energy to comfort friends through their online dating escapades. Simply put, she has bigger issues to worry about than petty, everyday problems. It may seem harsh, but in Capricorn's eyes, it's just the truth. Though not all sea goats fit this stereotype (she can even be extremely sensitive at times), Capricorn should remember that not every success in life can be featured on a resume, and ultimately, empathy is more important than any professional advancement. After all, it can get lonely at the top of the ladder. Compassion and ambition are not mutually exclusive, and when she is able to fuse these aspects of her life, she will be much happier.

Lessons in Love: Remember When...?

Capricorn has an excellent memory. If you say something once—even in passing—it will make a permanent imprint in your Capricorn partner's mind. This is great when it comes to remembering birthdays and anniversaries, but it definitely has its drawbacks...especially when you mention a present you purchased for an ex and later gift Capricorn a similar item by mistake. Yikes!

Checking the Boxes: Attracting Capricorn

Capricorn holds herself to a high standard, so she is attracted to partners who are equally ambitious. People who challenge her (whether it be through professional or creative talents, or even humor) catch her eye, so when you're courting Capricorn, be sure to double down on your best attributes. Emphasize your natural gifts and abilities, and Capricorn will definitely be interested.

Capricorn also aspires to create solid foundations for romantic bonds—so she doesn't want to waste time on superfluous relationships. To be blunt, Capricorn doesn't beat around the bush. If she is expressing interest, that means she *really* likes you. At first, her courtship style can seem fairly traditional. Expect dinner at no-frills restaurants, early-evening movie dates, and very, *very* minimal physical contact. The way she sees it, why waste time, money, or emotional energy on something if it's not going to work out? Until this sea goat can confirm a return on her investment, she will have a business-like attitude toward the courtship.

Should feelings develop, Capricorn will begin to warm up. Slowly, the sea goat will reveal her more hedonistic sensibilities: the restaurants will get swankier, and the nights will go on *much* later—perhaps even resulting in some spontaneous sleepovers. *Ooh la la.*

Boss in the Streets, Freak in the Sheets

The Capricorn lover approaches sex with determination and dedication. Things are extremely black-and-white for her when it comes to getting down: either it is an expression of a romantic dynamic—or it's just a casual hookup. When there isn't an emotional attachment, sex with Capricorn can at times be quite sterile, almost transactional. But, when she does want to let loose with someone she's emotionally attached to, this earthy lover showcases her inner freak (for example, her interest in consensual bondage and dirty talk). She should also explore role-playing with her lovers. This mentally freeing exercise allows her to venture into her mysterious sexual psyche, acting out fantasies that will surely bring her to her knees (the part of the body she just happens to rule in medical astrology).

In the context of sex, pleasure—both giving and receiving—becomes Capricorn's most *important* job. In fact, she prides herself on these sexual achievements—and aims to be "the best." In this vein, there is a competitive nature to Capricorn when it comes to sex. Don't be surprised if your Capricorn lover asks for a thorough recount of your sexual history. It may feel invasive, but she is merely trying to figure out what you haven't yet tried (so she can be your first) and what you have already experienced (so she can be the best).

Future Investment: Maintaining a Relationship with Capricorn

There's no doubt about it: Capricorn means business. Although she doesn't work for applause the way other signs do (ahem, Leo), she does demand respect and reverence—especially from her partner. Once a relationship moves past the initial courtship phase, Capricorn can begin to deepen the emotional connection, and it is here that her partner will hold up their end of the bargain. Capricorn needs to be with someone extremely trustworthy who will also play the role of a confidant. Don't forget: life isn't easy for this enterprising sea goat. Although she is focused on success, her determination comes from a psychological place. For this sign, work is necessary in order to *survive*. For Capricorn, work is a productive outlet for her inner struggles. So long as she keeps hustling, she can prevent all of her emotions from overpowering her logical approach to life. Obviously, this can become rather exhausting! So, in a committed relationship, Capricorn is extremely grateful for the opportunity to expose her vulnerabilities—securing not just a lover, but also a friend.

Written in the Stars

Capricorn isn't known for her volatile temper—but she does have a reputation for icy exits. If she feels betrayed, she won't explode. Instead, she'll methodically cut you out of her life, snipping each cord to ensure the bond is *never* rewired.

Overworked

Capricorn is known for her ambition and incredible endurance, and in a serious relationship she expects her partner's drive to match—or even exceed—her own. This desire isn't simply about being a power couple; it's also about building and maintaining a quality of life that steady Capricorn can depend on. Nothing is sexier to Capricorn than hard work. It's not uncommon, however, for the tenacious sea goat to project success onto her partner. She doesn't do this intentionally; it's just that she is *extremely* goal-oriented.

Here's an example: early into your relationship with Capricorn, you casually mention that you would like to own a house someday. At the time, this comment may not have had much thought behind it; you were simply making conversation. Capricorn, however, registered this remark as an objective. Gradually, she begins to ask more and more questions about your plan: What is your price range? Do you have a timeline? Have you familiarized yourself with interest rates? If you're unable to deliver thoughtful answers, Capricorn will start to believe that you're lazy and inactive—not her type at all. Alas, she has overworked an innocent comment.

When Capricorn pushes her partner too hard, resentment and discontent can arise on both sides. In order to avoid this, the sea goat must keep in mind that each person moves at their own pace and—perhaps more importantly—has their own definition of success. By the time Capricorn begins treating her significant other like an assistant, the relationship may be on its way out.

Difficult Business Matters

As the last earth sign, Capricorn approaches everything (including her romantic relationships) by analyzing data, reviewing the facts, and reaching a logical conclusion. If mutual needs in a relationship are satisfied, she is content and enjoys reaping the rewards. When the partnership is no longer productive, however, it's easy for this sea goat to justify any bad behavior on her part. And although she isn't particularly duplicitous, if Capricorn *does* decide to stray, she'll treat it as market research: she's simply exploring her options to figure out which type of bond is the most advantageous. At the end of the day, everything is a negotiation for this astrological entrepreneur; even the most emotional circumstances can be mitigated by a "good deal."

Make no mistake, if Capricorn believes a relationship has hope, she'll fight for it until the bitter end. But if she discovers that the math no longer adds up, she will prepare to close up shop. While certainly warmer than her reputation suggests, when it comes to breaking up, Capricorn excels at cord cutting. Simply put, this earth sign would rather accept the facts than delude herself. Moreover, she never, *ever* tries to convince someone to stay if they aren't interested in moving forward. For clear-eyed Capricorn, heartbreak is just another hard fact of life.

Sun Sign Love Matches

If you're lucky enough to snag Capricorn, you are guaranteed a stable, loyal, and encouraging partner. But she is also extremely straightforward. She has no time to play games; whereas for other signs, relationships are considered a sport. So, which astrological matches will Capricorn be willing to cosign with? In the following sections, you'll discover how this motivated sea goat interacts with each of the twelve signs of the zodiac.

Capricorn and Aries

Though both Capricorn and Aries are motivated and ambitious, these signs define success very differently. Capricorn, the mystical sea goat, slowly ascends the mountain, while Aries, the celestial ram, head-butts his way to the top. Truth be told, Aries's childlike exuberance can be off-putting to austere Capricorn: to her it seems sloppy and unrefined. Aries, meanwhile, may at times perceive Capricorn as uncreative and dull, wondering, "Why can't she just lighten up?" But don't fear! Not all hope is lost for these two enterprising signs. If they can learn to accept each other's logic, Capricorn and Aries can form a long-term partnership built on understanding and respect. Plus, these two have great sex—and that's definitely worth fighting for.

When Stars Align

Aries and Capricorn are both manifesters: these two signs are incredible at accomplishing their goals. When they work together—Aries offering the passion and Capricorn providing the structure—they have the ability to execute any idea. This is a great entrepreneurial pair!

Capricorn and Taurus

When it comes to celestial matchmaking, Capricorn and Taurus are an effortless pair. Taurus is smitten with Capricorn's focused dedication, as the determined sea goat offers the stability that the celestial bull craves. In addition, Capricorn appreciates Taurus's sensuality, which adds more nuanced layers to the sea goat's sometimes harsh tenacity. Capricorn and Taurus are both grounded, practical people, who truly understand each other. However, no relationship is *perfect*. In fact, Capricorn and Taurus can become too entrenched in their shared comfort zone. Relationships are supposed to be fun, so these two must be sure to keep the spark alive with a little spontaneity once in a while!

Capricorn and Gemini

Although this love combination may feel more like a mash-up than a blend, Capricorn and Gemini *can* form a dynamic partnership. In fact, these signs are *so* different that a romantic relationship between them is just crazy enough to work! Capricorn is intrigued by Gemini's seamless schmoozing, and Gemini wants to absorb all the wisdom Capricorn has to offer. Together, Capricorn and Gemini can teach each other invaluable lessons, inspiring each other professionally, creatively, and—of course—sexually along the way. Within this bond, Capricorn will also be sure to display her kinkier proclivities. All relationships require negotiation and compromise, of course, so if both of these signs are willing to invest in shared goals, Capricorn and Gemini have the potential to be lifelong partners.

Capricorn and Cancer

Opposites on the zodiac wheel, Capricorn and Cancer symbolize the celestial parents: Capricorn represents the masculine energy of the father, while Cancer is linked to the feminine energy of the mother. As the "dad" and "mom" of astrology, these signs share more traditional views on romance; thus, they aspire to build a safe domestic environment (the sea goat seeks solace in secluded caves, while the crab seeks comfort in her shell), filled with support, encouragement, and commitment. Of course, even the most devoted parents fight, so if Capricorn and Cancer plan to mate for life, they must be willing to accept the occasional scuffle. In the end, this bond is truly kismet.

Capricorn and Leo

Although neither sign wants to admit it, these two are secretly obsessed with each other. Capricorn is captivated by Leo's theatrical flair, and Leo is inspired by Capricorn's incredible work ethic. They have the potential to form an incredible power couple—but first, they need to be willing to release their egos. Specifically, Leo must accept that Capricorn's slow and steady approach sometimes *does* win the race, and Capricorn must acknowledge that Leo's drama is also—from time to time—an effective methodology. There will always be conflict in the Capricorn-Leo bond, but if they commit to a long-term partnership, this tension will become purely sexual...and both signs are very into that expression of their energy.

Capricorn and Virgo

Ambitious Capricorn works hard to build safety and security in her life. As a fellow earth sign, Virgo has similar aspirations (though sometimes she gets too caught up in nuance to create big-picture schemes). Accordingly, these signs make an incredible team. Capricorn appreciates Virgo's thoughtful organization, and Virgo admires

Capricorn's expansive vision. The Capricorn-Virgo couple is hardworking and rational. However, when it comes to romance, these two will need to make sure their dynamic doesn't become *too* practical: sometimes love is a bit wild! As long as both partners can find new ways to maintain a little sexy push and pull, these two can form a bond that is safe, secure, and built to last.

When Stars Align

Since Virgo focuses on details and Capricorn focuses on the big picture, these signs create a dynamic counterbalance that inspires innovation and forward motion. And because they both enjoy the outdoors, they'll love going on weekend getaways together. Virgo should just make sure to bring plenty of bug spray: this sign is often very sensitive to bites!

Capricorn and Libra

Capricorn is a workaholic. While some signs appreciate her steadfast ambition, this fastidious approach to life is certainly not for everyone. In a Capricorn-Libra bond, both signs need to work hard to make sure they are on the same page. Libra—the diplomat of the zodiac—can become frustrated by Capricorn's stoicism. As a hard worker, Capricorn doesn't have time for niceties—which are the very type of social interaction that propels Libra forward. Meanwhile, Capricorn easily gets annoyed by Libra's flippant, overly agreeable nature. When these two join forces, Capricorn must remember that Libra is *not* her assistant, and Libra must also accept his role as

Capricorn's loyal, dedicated partner. If they can learn to respect their differences, however, this will prove to be a successful and rewarding union.

Capricorn and Scorpio

In tarot, Scorpio is symbolized by the Death card and Capricorn by the Devil card. Unsurprisingly, the Scorpio-Capricorn bond is dark, mysterious...and extremely sexy. Scorpio is obsessed with power and control, but she meets her match with Capricorn. This mythical sea goat is so goal-oriented that nothing—not even Scorpio's seductive powers—can throw her off-balance. Of course, this is a huge turn-on for Scorpio, who works overtime to win Capricorn's hard-to-earn affection. Meanwhile, Capricorn sits back and relaxes: this earth sign loves to watch Scorpio sweat. While this push and pull is erotic, if these two want to cultivate a long-term relationship, they need to make sure their partnership isn't totally built on themes of dominance and submission. If the Capricorn-Scorpio match can occasionally let its hair down and have some fun, this romance may last forever.

When Stars Align

So what do Scorpio and Capricorn have in common? An interest in world domination! Both of these signs are extremely hardworking and resourceful, making them natural leaders (though, at their worst, horribly bossy).

Capricorn and Sagittarius

It's not always easy for signs who sit next to each other in the zodiac to date: they simply don't have a lot of perspective. This is certainly the case with Capricorn and Sagittarius. Optimistic Sagittarius makes Capricorn a bit uneasy, as she wonders, "Why can't this archer just stay focused?" Meanwhile, Capricorn's inherent pessimism disturbs Sagittarius, who works hard to enjoy life's many offerings. Ultimately, however, if a Capricorn-Sagittarius couple can learn how to work with—as opposed to *against*—each other, they can form a dynamic counterbalanced partnership that is simultaneously passionate and stable. It may take compromise, but, after all, everything in life is a negotiation.

Capricorn and Capricorn

How can a conference call turn into phone sex? Just ask the Capricorn-Capricorn pair. These two turn each other on with their work ethics, so it's very likely that they will first link up in a professional setting. However, this coupling is also relatively rare. Although Capricorns appreciate each other's ambition, sea goats tend to be quite guarded, making it nearly impossible for a Capricorn-Capricorn couple to break through the courtship phase. If these old souls can actually build a bond, however, they have the ability to form an unstoppable duo as one of the zodiac's fiercest, and perhaps most successful, power couples. Driven by their ambition, two Capricorns make for a full executive suite.

Capricorn and Aquarius

Dependable Capricorn and experimental Aquarius have completely different perspectives on life. Capricorn is rooted in reality. She rolls in "sensible" circles (she won't admit it, but she is extremely opportunistic) and cares deeply about her professional success. Aquarius, alternatively, thrives on ideas and lives to explore intellectual pursuits—often against the status quo. In fact, Aquarius wants to break the very mold Capricorn works hard to create. Naturally, there will be tension within this partnership, but Capricorn and Aquarius can also learn from each other. Although it may take a moment for each to appreciate the other's offerings, this couple has the potential for long-term compatibility.

Capricorn and Pisces

Capricorn's dedicated ambition and Pisces's wild creativity is a recipe for success. As a water sign, Pisces often has extremely artistic visions. However, she dwells in the ocean, so she lacks the grounding needed to transform her dreams into reality. Enter Capricorn, the magical sea goat. With the body of a goat and the tail of a fish, Capricorn is able to traverse both land (reality) and sea (subconscious), helping transport Pisces's abstract ideas to the material world. Capricorn must thoughtfully allocate her time between these two domains, however, and Pisces must give her the space to do so. If these signs can learn to navigate life together as a couple, their bond will be extremely rewarding.

Love Planets: Venus and Mars

While your Sun sign helps you understand the wants, needs, and special things that make you, well, *you*, it is just one component of your rich astrological profile. Your birth chart (a snapshot of the sky at your exact moment of birth) also features a number of planets, of which Venus and Mars will also reveal critical information about your romantic sensibilities. In astrology, Venus is linked to love, beauty, and money. By recognizing Venus's function in your astrological profile, you can unlock a deeper understanding of how you idealize partnership and approach your relationships. Mars, meanwhile, governs ambition, momentum, and sex. When exploring romantic compatibility, it's important to look at the role of Mars within your profile, as this placement offers insights into what you like and dislike in the bedroom. And, honestly, whether a relationship lasts one night or a lifetime, sexual attraction is a big part of the equation.

Venus in Capricorn

Capricorn may be the boss of the zodiac, but Venus in Capricorn is always seeking her proverbial "daddy." Venus's sensual energy is quelled by Capricorn's signature stoicism, but this planet finds its erotic outlet through experimenting with power dynamics. And because Capricorn believes strongly in work before play, Venus in Capricorn is turned on by sexual tension. But be warned, Venus in Capricorn will *not* waste her time with lazy lovers. If her partner can't deliver, she will leave—and never, ever look back. But more importantly, Venus in Capricorn seeks a romance that is a true partnership. For her, everything needs to be logical, and likewise, romance isn't just about matters of the heart; it's also a business she wants to see succeed.

Mars in Capricorn

Mars enjoys being in Capricorn's sky—in fact, this aggressive planet is "exalted" in this position, meaning it functions at its highest vibration when in Capricorn. Mars's impulsivity is tempered by Capricorn's signature restraint, enabling Mars in Capricorn to focus her energy exclusively on success (instead of being misguided by trademark Mars temper tantrums). Sexually, Mars in Capricorn is cool, calm, and collected...in an extremely erotic way. She will expect her lover to excel between the sheets. When in doubt, her partner should try some role-play: experimenting with power dynamics will be a serious turn-on.

Aquarius

(January 20–February 18)

Aquarius is often mistaken for a water sign due to the *aqua* prefix, but he is actually the last air sign of the zodiac. Air is associated with social movements, enhancing the qualities of the other elements (it ripples water, spreads fire, and sweeps up earth). Symbolized by the water bearer, who bestows life upon the land, Aquarius is the *quintessential* air sign. Progressive, rebellious, and revolutionary, he is here to shake up the establishment.

The Activist

Fervently supporting the concept of "power to the people," Aquarius believes in justice and equity. To this freethinker, everything is either social or political—and why shouldn't it be? He believes that every action has a reaction and, likewise, all of your choices reflect a corresponding moral. A rebel at heart, this air sign despises authority and is quick to reject *anything* that represents tradition or conventionality. He truly believes that shifts in perspective improve the greater good, and he isn't afraid to rattle a few cages where the good of the people is involved.

Written in the Stars

It's no surprise that so many groundbreaking thinkers were born under this sign: Abraham Lincoln, Thomas Edison, Rosa Parks, and Oprah Winfrey all embody the spirit of this humanitarian water bearer.

And don't even think about labeling Aquarius. As part of his rebellious nature, this air sign marches to the beat of his own drum, often trying out wacky clothing trends and unusual hobbies that others may shy away from. This eccentric way of life is quite inspiring to those around him, and he loves to prove that you can always dream bigger. If you've hit a roadblock in a project, ask Aquarius: his out-of-the-box thinking will surely produce some creative solutions.

The Whiz Kid

Aquarius is ruled by Uranus, the planet that governs innovation, technology, and shocking events (including earthquakes). You can always spot this sign by his gadgets: either he's hooked up with the most cutting-edge devices (the futuristic side of Aquarius), or he's intentionally using analog machinery from thirty years ago because he doesn't trust the government and/or corporations (the nihilistic side of Aquarius). He truly has a knack for advancement—which is why he is often called the whiz kid of the zodiac. Whip-smart and eager for change, he is always two steps ahead of modern society.

> **Written in the Stars**
> Uranus is quite unusual. It was the first planet discovered by a telescope (in 1781), and it is the only one named after a Greek deity. It is also tilted so far on its axis (a 98-degree angle) that it practically spins sideways.

And his love for technology and innovation doesn't stop with trendy gadgets: he is constantly trying to invent something of his own, whether it is a new type of utensil or a groundbreaking humanitarian organization. Whatever he pursues, he is always opinionated and virtuous, and he has very unusual ways of connecting with the world. Slow-moving Uranus is also associated with big, radical changes that impact entire generations, an energy that perfectly mirrors Aquarius's own punky attitude.

You Say You Want a Revolution: Aquarius Quirks

Aquarius is a fixed sign, meaning he was born at the height of a season (in his case, winter). As is the case with all fixed signs (Taurus, Leo, Scorpio, and Aquarius), he is seriously stubborn. And his obstinance is his true Achilles' heel (fittingly, in medical astrology, Aquarius governs the ankles). For instance, he may have once claimed that monogamy is impossible; however, after falling in love with the partner of his dreams, he knows he doesn't want to be with anyone else. Unfortunately, since he is so hardheaded, it may be difficult for him to admit that he was wrong, possibly causing some challenges within his relationship. Aquarius's persistence connects directly to his strong, righteous convictions, and fortunately this trait is quelled as soon as he gets the chance to enact positive, forward-moving change.

Since the water bearer is so motivated by egalitarianism, he enjoys engaging in teamwork and participating in communities of like-minded individuals. However, Aquarius still needs plenty of space to reflect, form ideas, and plan out his role within whatever revolution he's advocating. At the end of the day, freedom—both in theory and practice—is of the utmost importance to this sign. In fact, anyone who challenges Aquarius's independence is the enemy: a representation of society's power-hungry infrastructure designed to control the masses.

Aquarius won't hesitate to cut these "enemies" from his life. After all, he is more interested in society at large than in his own interpersonal relationships (he's all about the greater good). In fact, the water bearer can become so focused on implementing global change that he inadvertently neglects his family members and friends. It's not that he doesn't care—he's simply too preoccupied with large-scale social issues to plan a movie night. It is important in these instances to remind Aquarius that progress always starts on a smaller scale: before you can expect change to occur in the masses, you need to implement empathy within your own immediate reality. And sure, attending to a loved one's wants and needs may not save the world—but it *will* save the relationship.

Joining the Revolution: Attracting Aquarius

As you can imagine, it's not easy to court Aquarius, as he is so focused on society as a whole, and not small talk with one person. However—although he hates to admit it—he is a warm-blooded creature who wants affection too. Because Aquarius is not a particularly physical being (as an air sign and forward thinker, he is extremely cerebral), romance tends to look a lot like friendship for the water bearer. This may limit the ways you can showcase your interest in him, but Aquarius actually prefers it that way (you can leave the GMO, preservative-laden chocolates at home, thank you very much).

Aquarius loves thinking outside of the box, so his approach to dating is relaxed and—surprise, surprise—

unconventional. Rather than the traditional dinner-and-a-movie date, consider something that suits his personal interests (for instance, a robot-making workshop or trip to a quirky museum). But also remember this: Aquarius believes that every single interest, hobby, and activity needs to reflect an individual's ethics, so make sure to find out *exactly* what he enjoys before making any reservations.

Lessons in Love: What Should You Gift Aquarius?

As you continue getting to know Aquarius, ask him questions about the causes that matter most to him. Are there certain groups or nonprofits he finds inspiring? For his birthday or your anniversary, you should consider making a donation to one of these organizations. Since Aquarius is not particularly motivated by material possessions, your philanthropy is the best gift of all.

Perhaps the most important thing to know about romancing Aquarius, however, is that he needs personal space—and a lot of it. Alone time is absolutely essential for this sign. In fact, he will revolt if he feels claustrophobic. When in doubt, back off and let Aquarius come to you. Remember, although he is aloof, the truth is that he does care a lot—he just has his own unique way of expressing these feelings.

Lessons in Love: Is Aquarius Faithful?
Many signs may take his need for sovereignty as a sign of duplicity, but it's the complete opposite: Aquarius makes an extremely loyal partner. To him, independence and fidelity are not mutually exclusive. In fact, this air sign believes that in order to have a healthy, stable relationship, both individuals need to maintain their own sense of identity.

Express Yourself

Aquarius is an eccentric, so he is attracted to progressive, funky clothing styles. Asymmetrical haircuts, mismatched shoes, and hemp-based accessories are staples for this forward-thinking air sign. And since he is doing his own thing aesthetically, he wants his partner to be rocking something wild too! Aquarius *hates* to be labeled and categorized, so he is especially turned on by people who have offbeat styles that blend different looks: one-part hippie, one-part goth, one-part disco yields Aquarius's dream mate. Take advantage of your crush on this sign by trying out that whimsical ensemble you've been too nervous to wear in the past!

Making (Physical) Contact

Aquarius is totally out of this world: he is truly the "alien" of the zodiac. With his head so high up in the clouds, it's no surprise that this air sign has a reputation for being a bit detached when it comes to intimacy. However, though he is often more concerned with the abstract realm than with carnal desires, don't be fooled: Aquarius is no stranger to pleasure—and he *definitely* knows what he wants.

Everything about Aquarius is unconventional, so it's no surprise that he enjoys intimacy that doesn't follow a script. Turn your Aquarius lover on by switching up the roles, experimenting with hidden desires, and exploring new ways of expressing your individual (and shared) sexuality. And because Aquarius rules the ankles, this upside-down thinker will enjoy being flipped in the sheets with a little 69 action. Also, consider incorporating toys into your sexual vernacular. Since Aquarius is associated with technology, the latest pleasure gadgets will be sure to stimulate more than his imagination.

Embrace Change: Maintaining a Relationship with Aquarius

Aquarius builds relationships with passionate people who share his values, so friends can often become romantic partners for Aquarius, and these close connections can transform overnight. Although it may be difficult to balance his need for independence with the needs of the relationship, when Aquarius commits, he understands that everything is a negotiation. Fundamentally, he wants things to be fair, not for his particular preferences to dominate the bond. So when cultivating a partnership with Aquarius, experiment with creating different parameters together. Maybe you decide that he can turn his phone to airplane mode for a few hours each night to create a sense of freedom, or perhaps you spend a weekend apart every six months. Remember that space apart doesn't necessarily mean emotional distance. Sometimes a bit of separation can actually help deepen the love and trust, laying the foundation for a truly concrete relationship.

It is also important to keep in mind that even though Aquarius expresses his emotions in unusual ways, he *does* have feelings—and a lot of them. He does his best to be a thoughtful and kind partner, and when he is in need, he'll depend on the support of his relationship (and his whole community). He may not be able to communicate his sensitivities, but trust that things can be painful for Aquarius, and he needs time to heal from hurt just like any other sign. When the going gets tough, remind him that he always has a shoulder to cry on. He may not take you up on the offer, but he'll be comforted to know how deeply you care.

A Better Tomorrow

Though Aquarius is playful and inspiring within his relationships, he is sure to exhibit his signature aloofness during a breakup. He isn't petty: he doesn't care who breaks up with whom. At the end of the day, if a relationship isn't working, he'll simply accept the loss and hope for a better tomorrow. Indeed, he approaches separation from a highly intellectual, almost clinical perspective. The newly single Aquarian will spend hours analyzing the relationship's successes and failures—he may even discover published studies that support his scholarly theories. This approach to heartache may seem cold and disconnected to those around him, but it's the only way this air sign knows how to cope.

Sun Sign Love Matches

There's no doubt about it: Aquarius loves shock value. He is always ready and willing to fight for a humanitarian cause, but if you rub this hardheaded air sign the wrong way, *you* may very well become the problem. So, will you join Aquarius's revolution? Read on to discover the distinctive ways this eccentric sign interacts with each sign of the zodiac—the answers may surprise you.

Aquarius and Aries

There's an interesting dynamic between Aquarius and Aries, namely because both of these signs march to the beat of their own drum. Neither Aquarius nor Aries wants to be limited by social conventions, so they appreciate each other's independence. However, this partnership may require a bit of adjusting to see the full potential of this dynamic. Aquarius may get frustrated by Aries's self-centered perspective, and Aries may feel unappreciated due to Aquarius's signature aloofness. The Aquarius-Aries bond will benefit most from communication, so both partners should be willing to be vulnerable in their verbal expression. If Aquarius and Aries can continue to remind each other *why* they invest in each other, they can create a healthy relationship that is built to last.

Aquarius and Taurus

Aquarius and Taurus are without a doubt the two most stubborn signs of the zodiac: the celestial water bearer is self-righteous, and the cosmic bull is old-fashioned. Indeed, these two can really push each other's buttons. Rebellious Aquarius dislikes Taurus's adoration of tradition, and Taurus feels attacked by Aquarius's strict morality. If these signs do decide to partner, they will need to learn how to appreciate each other's differences—which is not an easy feat for such obstinate signs. However, Aquarius can learn how to appreciate the earthly realm, while Taurus can practice being more tolerant of different worldviews. This relationship will not be easy, but if the love is strong, these two can make it work.

Aquarius and Gemini

Symbolized by the water bearer, Aquarius is known for his humanitarianism. This air sign enjoys big-picture thinking and is motivated by social work that inspires progress. As a fellow air sign, Gemini admires Aquarius's revolutionary spirit, which also sets the stage for the chatty twin to perform. Aquarius, meanwhile, enjoys Gemini's more lighthearted spirit: in an unusual display, he actually has *fun* in this bond. Through dynamic ideating and clever banter, the Aquarius-Gemini partnership is truly electric. Although this duo must work hard to remain grounded (after all, the relationship is all air), when Aquarius and Gemini commit, they invest together in the greater good.

When Stars Align

There are not many signs that can make Aquarius laugh, but Gemini truly brings out his playful sensibilities. Some of Aquarius's stiff, fixed air is diffused by Gemini's lightness. Even better, these signs don't just bring out the best in each other; they're also extremely fun to be around! With this couple, a friend will never feel like a third wheel.

Aquarius and Cancer

This partnership isn't *impossible*, but it certainly isn't the most *probable*. Cancer will always put friends and family first, whereas Aquarius...well, just doesn't see community in the same way. For him, it is about the greater good of the whole world. Everything is socially or politically charged for the water bearer, so he's willing to abandon his comfort zone in order to prove a point. This horrifies Cancer, who can't even fathom the notion of intentionally leaving her own comfort zone. However, while Cancer is more focused on her immediate domain, both of these signs are innovative thinkers with bright ideas. Though it may be exceptionally difficult, with the right balance of honesty and understanding, Aquarius and Cancer can join forces. And as to whether these two will last? That will have to be left to the stars.

Aquarius and Leo

When Aquarius bonds with Leo, the combination of air and fire makes for a surprisingly fantastic match.

Aquarius helps temper Leo's ego, and Leo shows Aquarius that it's okay to infuse a bit of glamour into his world every now and then. And since Leo represents the ruler and Aquarius symbolizes the people, this couple has a comprehensive understanding of complex social systems. However, Leo is all heart and Aquarius is all brain (Leo is actually associated in medical astrology with the heart). This is an extremely important distinction, because Aquarius's signature detached nature can threaten Leo's pride, whereas Leo's dramatic outbursts can rub Aquarius the wrong way. Fortunately, if Aquarius and Leo can meet in the middle—Aquarius by being a little more affectionate, and Leo by being a bit less theatrical—these two can create a beautiful counterbalance that yields a lasting bond.

Aquarius and Virgo

There are some distinctive differences between Aquarius and Virgo (air signs are inspired by the abstract, whereas earth signs are driven by reality), but interestingly they create a unique bond. Virgo helps Aquarius understand nuance, while Aquarius encourages Virgo to explore the big picture. The most profound issue that these two will have to overcome is their extremely different relationships with authority. While Virgo hates to break rules, Aquarius *lives* for the opportunity to challenge the establishment. When coupled, this dissonance can make both partners quite uneasy. However, if they can each learn to understand the other's perspective, Aquarius and Virgo can form a special relationship.

When Stars Align

Aquarius *hates* being labeled—but labeling is what Virgo does best. Because of this, there are some serious tensions in the Virgo-Aquarius bond, but if Aquarius can learn to understand Virgo's categorical mind, it will be easier for these two to build a sustainable partnership. After all, Virgo isn't trying to put Aquarius in a box: she just sees the world through a very structured lens.

Aquarius and Libra

When Aquarius and Libra match up, is the bond real—or are they just blowing hot air? When these two air signs join forces, it's hard to tell whether they're pairing up for sex, love, or social status. Although Aquarius will never admit that he is opportunistic, both signs are hyperaware of their social networks. Libra, of course, wants to be well liked, and Aquarius wants to prove a point. While Aquarius and Libra effortlessly understand each other, each partner needs to make sure that he's investing in the relationship for the right reasons. Otherwise, this connection will likely fade into the ethers.

When Stars Align

Libra hates to argue (his mantra is "Can't we all just get along?"), while Aquarius loves a good challenge. In fact, Aquarius definitely provokes Libra, which can get under Libra's skin. Through this relationship, Libra learns that not all relationships are created equal. It's not important to be liked by everyone; what matters is being respected by those who share his values.

Aquarius and Scorpio

It is well known that Scorpio is associated with sex: the celestial scorpion just oozes eroticism. Aquarius, however, is not *nearly* as carnal. It's not that Aquarius isn't horny—the water bearer is definitely hot-blooded—it's just that he has a very distinctive approach to sexuality. Aquarius is intrigued by experimentation, whereas Scorpio is all about the art of seduction. This discrepancy reveals the tension between these two signs: they just have totally different ways of getting down. However, if they can learn to work together and invest in their passion and mutual attraction, the Aquarius-Scorpio bond is indestructible. Both fiercely loyal, they are willing to commit to each other for life.

Aquarius and Sagittarius

There's incredible harmony between Aquarius and Sagittarius: represented by air and fire, respectively, they create a union that's vibrant and dynamic. Aquarius inspires Sagittarius to fuse his love of philosophy with social justice, while Sagittarius encourages Aquarius to become more social. Together, these two signs have all the makings for an extremely powerful couple that can *actually* change the world. However, in order for Aquarius and Sagittarius to maintain a romantic relationship, they need to make sure they're also spending one-on-one time together. Neither of these signs is particularly motivated by partnership, so it may be difficult for them to form a lasting bond. But if they're willing to sprinkle their crowd-stirring with the occasional snuggle-sesh, it will *definitely* be worth their while.

Aquarius and Capricorn

Sensible, hardworking Capricorn is rooted in the here and now—namely her professional pursuits. Aquarius, on the other hand, thrives on the abstract, seeking new ideas and unique intellectual opportunities—quite often against the status quo. As Aquarius works to break the mold that Capricorn has strived to create, tension will arise between the signs. Fortunately, there is also a lot that Capricorn and Aquarius can learn from each other. Natural-born leaders, both the sea goat and the water bearer will come to appreciate what the other has to offer...it will just take a bit of patience and open communication.

Aquarius and Aquarius

An Aquarius-Aquarius couple works because each partner appreciates the other's similar ideologies, eccentric style, and forward-thinking attitude. Somehow, Aquarius is able to fall in love—without any earthly grounding. However, these two may have a hard time building a lasting bond simply because it *is* so difficult, if not impossible, for them to remain anchored. Aquarius loves without being attached, which can be tough when pairing up. Depending on personal preferences, one or both signs may need a partner who's a bit more down-to-earth (or even just *on* earth in the first place). The good news is that they can feed off of each other's quirkiness, and each understands the other's particular Aquarian sensitivity, which other people often misunderstand.

Aquarius and Pisces

While Aquarius spends the day writing manifestos, Pisces prefers to pen poetry. However, despite their different styles of expression, both Aquarius and Pisces are humanitarians who see a situation and immediately wonder, "What can I do to make this better?" Of course, Aquarius's ultraheady, intellectual approach, though admirable, is foreign to intuitive Pisces, who is primarily motivated by emotion. Likewise, Pisces's gentle touch is surprising to Aquarius, who moves through life with cool detachment. While the Aquarius-Pisces match starts off strong, each partner must work to accommodate the other's distinctive needs: Aquarius will need Pisces to inspire, while Pisces will need Aquarius to show he cares.

Love Planets: Venus and Mars

Your Sun sign helps you understand the desires, needs, and other little quirks that make up your essence; it is just one component of your astrological profile. Your birth chart (a snapshot of the sky at your exact moment of birth) features a number of planets, each with its own purposes. Of these, Venus and Mars reveal critical information about your romantic sensibilities. In astrology, Venus is linked to love, beauty, and money. You can look to Venus to understand the way you idealize partnership and approach relationships. Mars, on the other hand, governs ambition, momentum, and sex. The placement of Mars in your chart will reveal key insights into how you like to "get down." And, let's be honest, whether a relationship lasts one night or an entire lifetime, sexual attraction is a big piece of the puzzle.

Venus in Aquarius

Aquarius energy is eccentric, progressive, and detached. Accordingly, Venus in Aquarius is smitten with nonconformity. In fact, for this partner, the perfect relationship cannot be defined, because he refuses to classify any interpersonal connection through social conventions. Accordingly, Venus in Aquarius is drawn to free-spirited individuals who exist in the gray area between lover and friend. When it comes to matters of the heart, this quirky partner definitely lets his freak flag fly.

Mars in Aquarius

Aquarius is motivated to make radical shifts with the potential to impact many people, so Mars in Aquarius isn't at all interested in small, single-minded tasks. In fact, it's not easy for him to find motivation, simply because most day-to-day endeavors don't have a global impact. When Mars in Aquarius does find his calling, however, he is absolutely unstoppable. He is also linked to technological innovation, so he loves to explore sexuality with an industrial twist. He is especially drawn to toys, so don't be surprised if your Mars in Aquarius lover busts out a treasure chest filled with pleasure devices.

Chapter 12

Pisces

(February 19–March 20)

Pisces is symbolized by two fish swimming in opposite directions, connected by a single, invisible string—a representation of her existence at the intersection of fantasy and reality. Indeed, as the final sign of the zodiac, Pisces has absorbed every lesson learned by the preceding eleven signs. All of their joys, pains, and hopes are at her fingertips. Accordingly, she is the most psychic and empathetic sign in the astrological wheel. Sweet and gentle, but elusive like a sea creature, she dwells in deep waters.

The Mist

Pisces is governed by Neptune, the distant celestial body that oversees creativity and dreams, as well as illusion and escapism. Indeed, Neptune is beautiful, beguiling...and sometimes scary. On earth, when a haze rolls across the ocean, the horizon is obstructed, and there's no distinction between sky and water. Likewise, Neptune can either be enchantingly romantic (think of walking in the mist on a romantic evening) or terrifyingly dangerous (imagine trying to drive a car through dense fog).

Written in the Stars

Did you know that Pisces (and her planetary ruler, Neptune) is associated with the entertainment industry? It's no surprise, then, that some of its most influential figures, including Elizabeth Taylor, Desi Arnaz, and Liza Minnelli, were born under this sky. Perhaps it's the emotional range...

These attributes are also reflected within Pisces. As a water sign, she has an extremely multidimensional depth and mystical allure that make her quite captivating to others. Much like an ocean, she alternates between smooth waters and massive waves. One day, she is quite serene, dreaming about the future and reflecting on the people and events in her life. The next, she is intense and turbulent, unleashing her deep sensitivities in great, sweeping motions. It's important to remember that the ocean *is* an extremely powerful force. So, before you set sail, make sure you're prepared for the full range of temperaments ahead.

The Flexible Fish

As a mutable sign, Pisces is born at the transition from a season (in her case, winter). Mutable signs (Gemini, Virgo, Sagittarius, and Pisces) are flexible, ready and willing to go with the flow—wherever it leads. True to form, Pisces is never afraid to change her mind. In fact, she relishes the opportunity to adopt new points of view. One day, Pisces may find herself in a conflict with a close companion; the next day, she has completely erased the drama from memory and is already moving on.

Pisces also encourages others to see life from new perspectives, and you can count on this caring water sign to help you tap into these foreign points of view. Hesitant to move away from what you know? Pisces has your back! She understands just how eye-opening these experiences can be. In fact, she is always looking for new ways to broaden her horizons. Whether she's seeing the world through a camera lens or a kaleidoscope, Pisces loves activating her spiritualty through mind-altering experiences—even if it means occasionally following a white rabbit down a mysterious hole. As the last sign of the zodiac, she knows that reality is truly subjective.

The Emotional Sponge: Pisces Quirks

Otherworldly Pisces can pick up on the energies, auras, and nonverbal expressions of those around her. In fact, this sign is quite the emotional sponge, absorbing absolutely everything in her environment—including whatever exists in the ethereal plane. With such immense empathy,

Pisces can easily become swallowed by her sensitives, so this sea creature must work hard to stay grounded. One way to do this is through body scans. Your body can tell you a lot about what you are feeling mentally and how those feelings manifest in palpable ways. Before Pisces enters a new situation, she should take a moment to reflect on how she is feeling physically, noting any pains, itches, or discomforts. Then, when she leaves the situation, she should perform the same exercise once more. Does everything feel the same, or do certain body parts (for instance, her head or stomach) feel changed? If things feel different, she has probably absorbed someone else's energy. When Pisces becomes aware of where she holds tension, it will be easier for her to identify how the feelings of others affect her physically. From here, she can focus on establishing boundaries to avoid being overwhelmed by everyone else's problems in the future.

Under the Sea: Attracting Pisces

Pisces is a gentle, kind, and artistic soul who is invigorated by dreams, music, and—perhaps most importantly—love. Dating a Pisces is like diving into the deepest parts of the vast ocean: it's exciting, refreshing, and extremely mysterious. In fact, Pisces is directly associated with the siren: a beautiful sea creature who lures sailors to their deaths with her songs. Of course, this association is *purely* literary (there are no such fatalities associated with Pisces), but still, Pisces is truly enchanting—even to herself!

Pisces is particularly drawn to artistic types. This sensitive fish has unparalleled access to the collective unconscious through her clairvoyance, making her incredibly receptive to art. She is looking for a partner who can match her creative eye. And being an imaginative sign, Pisces also gravitates toward unusual people who march to the beat of their own drums. It's not that her ideal match is a social outcast, however; she actually prefers partners who are embedded in hip, progressive communities. She personally loves to travel in a school of like-minded fish (she is symbolized by this scaly sea creature, after all), so the more friends someone has, the more interested she will be in them.

When it comes to date night with Pisces, consider checking out a concert, touring an art district, or even enrolling in a pottery workshop. She is invigorated by shared experiences—especially those that involve nonverbal, nonmaterial domains. Indeed, any experience with mystical Pisces is guaranteed to involve deep spiritual exploration. And because she is *so* incredibly sensitive to her surroundings, she is greatly impacted by external stimuli. As an emotional sponge, she takes everything in, after all: the good, the bad, and the ugly—it's a lot to digest! Over time, you can figure out exactly what types of experiences your Pisces partner can and cannot tolerate. But in the beginning of your courtship, avoid anything overly stimulating: no spicy food, no horror movies, and *definitely* no stand-up comedy. This sensitive creature cannot stand anything mean-spirited, so if the comedian's jokes are nasty, it can upset her deeply.

Mermaid Sex

With this extremely psychic and emotional characterization, Piscean intercourse is deeply spiritual. This deep-sea mermaid understands intimacy as the coming together of two unique, exquisite souls: the true definition of making love. So, although she *can* have casual sex, Pisces prefers to "get down" with someone she cares for deeply. After all, this sensitive sign has a difficult time establishing boundaries: borders don't exist in the sea.

Slippery When Wet

Through the act of intercourse, Pisces can become seduced by her own fantasies. The sheets become waves, and the bed transforms into a vast, limitless ocean. Indeed, Pisces dives headfirst into sensuality. She also rules the feet, which (like Pisces's own deep soul) carry the weight of the world. Accordingly, a steamy foot massage serves as excellent foreplay. And when it comes to the physical act of making love, Pisces will love exploring tantric sex, focusing on the harmony and rhythm of her breath and movement with her lover's. Through this highly erotic, sensual experience, Pisces can venture between her physical body and her subconscious mind. So, if the bond is karmic or from a past life, this expression of intimacy will help her and her lover transcend into alternate dimensions.

Navigating the Tides: Maintaining a Relationship with Pisces

While casually dating Pisces feels like journeying into another dimension—beguiling, but still easy to come up for air—it's much harder to navigate her tides within a committed relationship. In fact, creating a long-term partnership with Pisces is an art in and of itself: it takes bravery, strength, and adaptability.

Lessons in Love: What Should You Gift Pisces?

Pisces is a dreamer, known for her extremely vivid subconscious world. A great present for your Pisces partner is a dream journal (and nice pen!) that she can keep by her bed. That way, she can start tracking the amazing ways her imagination manifests and the ideas it sparks for her material life. Who knows? She may be the next Steve Jobs!

Pisces operates in her own reality—so it's no wonder that this imaginative water sign can be a bit flaky. For instance, she may discuss settling down with a family early on in a relationship, only to change her mind several months later. She also may get cold feet before making any major purchases, such as buying property, or merging bank accounts. There are no limits in the ocean, after all, so Pisces has an aversion to things being set in stone. If she can avoid it, she'd rather not have too many responsibilities!

While it may be frustrating, it's nearly impossible to confront Pisces about her unreliable behavior: because she lacks emotional armor (like Cancer's shell or Scorpio's exoskeleton), her only defense is to swim away. Indeed, Pisces tends to abandon ship at even the *slightest* criticism. In a relationship, Pisces must remember that her partner's feelings need to be shared. It may be hard for her to accept something she doesn't want to hear, but communication is the key to making sure the relationship isn't lost at sea. If you do feel like your Pisces mate is beginning to drift away, a great way to bring her back to the shore is through music (her favorite creative outlet). It may seem simple, but tickets to her favorite rock band or a customized playlist will definitely capture her heart and help restore her faith in your bond.

Written in the Stars

Pisces is such a sensitive soul, so from an early age she often develops her own coping system. If your Pisces partner ever behaves a bit oddly during an argument or tough time, understand that these are the skills she has developed in order to create stability. This ethereal creature is impacted by *everything*, so it's important for her to set boundaries!

However, should a relationship reach the point of no return, Pisces will retreat silently into the horizon. She would rather not deal with conflict, so her preferred style of breaking up is often vague and inconclusive. After all, because she exists within the abstract realm, clear boundaries are not her strong suit. Instead of establishing a conclusive ending, she will quietly float away from the relationship, leaving more questions than answers in her wake.

Sun Sign Love Matches

Because she is the last sign of the zodiac, dating Pisces is no small feat: there's a lot of responsibility when it comes to courting such a gentle, psychic creature! So how can you tell which astrological matches will float and which will sink? Grab a life jacket! In the following sections, you'll explore how Pisces interacts in a romantic relationship with each zodiac sign.

When Stars Align

Aries governs the head, while Pisces rules the feet. Obviously, there's a lot in between these two domains: a representation of everything the Pisces-Aries couple must reconcile in order to form a long-lasting bond. It won't be easy, but in the end, these two complete each other.

Pisces and Aries

When the last sign of the zodiac pairs up with the first sign, the results can be a bit unpredictable. Pisces, as the final incarnation, is infused with wisdom and emotion. Aries, on the other hand, is just getting started; fire energy is eager, innocent, and—perhaps most importantly—selfish. Aries's ego isn't a bad thing, though; after all, it motivates him to take action. But when he is partnered with Pisces (who is undoubtedly the *most* selfless sign), these different ideologies can feel disjointed and off-balance. However, if Pisces can accept Aries's brutishness as part of his naiveté, and Aries can embrace Pisces's gentle soul, the Aries-Pisces match can be a dynamic pairing, fueled by knowledge and mutual respect.

Pisces and Taurus

Pisces and Taurus are both romantics, which is why these two signs form an instant attraction. Pisces loves art and poetry, while Taurus adores food and wine; together, their bond is a fully Venusian experience (Venus is, in fact, "exalted" in Pisces). Interestingly, however, what keeps Pisces and Taurus linked is not their shared hedonism; it's their ability to teach each other critical lessons. Pisces helps earthy Taurus understand abstract ideas, while Taurus encourages emotional Pisces to anchor herself a bit more in reality. Together, these signs are more than romantic partners: they're also each other's muses. Although this relationship will need to work out certain kinks (Pisces can be flighty, and Taurus can be possessive), it is extremely powerful.

Pisces and Gemini

There's really nothing *wrong* in the Pisces-Gemini bond—except for its difficulty in sustaining itself. It's a funny thing, actually, how compatible these water and air signs are on the surface: Pisces is attracted to Gemini's social prowess, while Gemini is enchanted by Pisces's effortless creativity. However, both of these mutable signs are fueled by duality (Pisces is symbolized by two fish, and Gemini by the twins), so they are constantly being pulled in opposite directions. Just as easily as they are drawn together, they're also pulled apart. Accordingly, in order for the Pisces-Gemini bond to last, these signs will need to commit to the same motion. Although both are inclined to run away, sticking around for this electric relationship may be the best decision either sign ever makes.

Pisces and Cancer

Pisces is truly otherworldly. Known for her sweet disposition, endearing creativity, and powerful clairvoyance, this deep-sea fish absorbs energies, auras, and all that exists within the gray areas of life. Cancer, also an aquatic creature, is a great match for Pisces. Unlike the deep-sea fish, the celestial crustacean is also able to walk on land, so Pisces's relationship with this fellow water sign can be both emotionally rewarding *and* extremely grounding. At the same time, Cancer can learn from Pisces how to hone her own intuitive skills. Of course, things can get a bit slippery from time to time (especially when Cancer snaps her claws and Pisces swims away), but as long as they lead with empathy and compassion, this duo can definitely get deep.

Pisces and Leo

Pisces and Leo are both amazingly creative, albeit through different forms of expression. While Leo enjoys taking center stage, Pisces loves to create abstract works that reflect her own multidimensionality. When coupled, these signs can function as each other's muses, inspiring the other to continue cultivating their own artistic gifts.

However, water and fire can also be destructive: Pisces's pool of emotions is evaporated by Leo's blinding theatrics, and Leo's flame is dampened by Pisces's sensitivity. Indeed, it will take work for the Pisces-Leo pairing to last: both partners will need to learn how to accommodate the other's intrinsic needs. But if they're willing, this relationship can be imaginative and deeply inspiring.

When Stars Align

Between Leo's theatrics and Pisces's creativity, these two can form an extraordinarily dynamic duo. After all, since Pisces and her planetary ruler Neptune govern the entertainment industry, Leo's performative spirit will gravitate toward this watery lover. Lucille Ball (Leo) and Desi Arnaz (Pisces) perfectly embody the essence of this pair.

Pisces and Virgo

Both Pisces and Virgo are sensitive and compassionate, so these opposite signs relate to each other on a deeply empathetic level. Within this gentle partnership, Pisces and Virgo aspire to bring out the best in each other and, in doing so, create a beautiful and stable bond. Virgo's logical mind helps wandering Pisces achieve her goals, while Pisces's creative ingenuity inspires Virgo to explore her own artistic expression. However, while Pisces and Virgo can benefit from each other's kindness and support, problems may develop when these signs become martyrs. What they need to remember is that relationships are more about compromise than sacrifice. If each sign spends the entire partnership bleeding out, there won't be anything left to celebrate.

Pisces and Libra

Venus (who is, in fact, "exalted" in Pisces) oversees the Pisces-Libra relationship, and for these two, their meeting can truly feel like love at first sight. Indeed, sensitive Pisces and thoughtful Libra are both hopeless romantics, so they gravitate instantly toward this cosmic expression of love. *Hopeless* is a keyword, however: while Pisces and Libra *want* to create a successful bond, neither are quite sure how to sustain their union long term. Since neither sign is particularly decisive, it's easier for these two to crush on each other from afar. Further, both Pisces and Libra *hate* conflict, so when the going gets tough, they, well, get going. If Pisces and Libra want to cultivate a lasting relationship, they will need to create goals, set boundaries, and communicate their respective needs—even if that means the occasional argument.

Pisces and Scorpio

The bond between Pisces and Scorpio is often profoundly spiritual. Scorpio is notoriously secretive, and while most other signs have a difficult time accepting her interest in privacy, Pisces is happy to respect these boundaries. In fact, because Pisces is so innately psychic, she actually doesn't *need* Scorpio to share personal information: she can access everything she needs to know through nonverbal communication. Scorpio, of course, truly appreciates this and, with a fierce exoskeleton, can help teach Pisces how to advocate for her own needs. However, since

Pisces needs lots of space to explore and Scorpio tends to be quite possessive, these two will still need to figure out their rhythm. But, at the end of the day, Pisces and Scorpio make for a dynamic, supportive, and truly enchanting couple.

When Stars Align

Neither Pisces nor Scorpio is scared of the other's darker side. In fact, this partnership teaches each sign how to self-soothe. Kurt Russell (Pisces) and Goldie Hawn (Scorpio) have been together since 1983—a true testament to the strength of this bond!

Pisces and Sagittarius

Pisces and Sagittarius instantly understand each other, as they are both wanderers. Though as a water sign and a fire sign, respectively, they explore different realms: Pisces is linked to the ocean (which symbolizes emotions) and Sagittarius's flames ignite the land (an expression of philosophy and academia). When these two come together, they provide each other with important information about their distinctive domains. Indeed, Pisces and Sagittarius inspire each other, fueling mutual interests. However, they may struggle to stay partnered for very long: Pisces needs water to stay vibrant, and Sagittarius requires firm ground to keep his fire burning bright. In order for Pisces and Sagittarius to last in a romantic relationship, they will need to accept their distance and give each other freedom to roam.

Pisces and Capricorn

Usually, water and earth signs meet in happy harmony—but in the case of Pisces and Capricorn, the bond can get a bit muddy. Pisces is incredibly emotional and sensitive, whereas Capricorn is mainly fueled by the practical, physical world. In most cases, such differences can inspire; however, when it comes to Pisces and Capricorn, Pisces may feel stifled by Capricorn's rigidity, and Capricorn can be put off by Pisces's lack of grounding. Fortunately, these two can learn to work together, as Pisces can share her creativity with enterprising Capricorn, and Capricorn can offer the structure to help Pisces see her dreams through to reality.

When Stars Align

Pisces and Capricorn form a bond known as "sextile." In astrology, sextiles occur when either earth energy fuses with water energy, or fire energy fuses with air energy, in modalities different to each other.

Pisces and Aquarius

The last two signs of the zodiac, Pisces and Aquarius make an interesting couple. When Aquarius's powerful air energy fuses with Pisces's expansive waters, hurricanes are to be expected. In the eye of the storm, however, Pisces and Aquarius actually form a dynamic alignment: both signs are interested in exploring the mysteries of life, and although Aquarius is linked to science and Pisces to spirituality, they each have a deep appreciation for the other's perspective. These two can entertain each other endlessly by sharing their abstract theories, philosophies, and ideologies. While it may be difficult for Pisces and Aquarius to push past the whirlwinds, at the end of the day, they make an excellent team.

Pisces and Pisces

This isn't a couple: it's a school of fish! Pisces and Pisces are both dreamers—romantic, poetic, and sensitive—so this bond is primarily based on spirituality and creativity. In fact, because Pisces is so psychic, this relationship may seem karmic; perhaps it's a past-life partnership. But there are no boundaries in the ocean, and likewise, it's difficult for these two to define their romantic identity. If and when they do, however, the Pisces-Pisces relationship can become a bit *too* submerged in emotion: it's easy for these fish to become codependent and thus a bit self-destructive. If they want to create a healthy, sustainable bond, they will need to figure out how to build a solid infrastructure around their shapeless sensitivities. Most importantly, these two will need to learn how to balance care for themselves with care for each other.

Love Planets: Venus and Mars

Your Sun sign helps you understand your essence (the wants, needs, and special things that make you, well, *you*), which is extremely important in exploring romantic compatibility. However, this sign is just one component of your rich, complex astrological profile. Your birth chart (a snapshot of the sky at your exact moment of birth) features a number of planets—each embedded with its own functions and purposes. Of these, Venus and Mars reveal critical information about your romantic sensibilities. In astrology, Venus is linked to love, beauty, and money. By understanding Venus's function in your astrological profile, you can unlock the secrets of how you idealize partnership and approach your relationships. Mars, meanwhile, governs ambition, momentum, and sex. When exploring romantic compatibility, it's important to look at the role of Mars within your profile, as this placement offers insights into your preferences between the sheets. And, honestly, whether a relationship lasts for one night or a lifetime, sexual attraction is a major part of the equation.

Venus in Pisces

The last sign of the zodiac, Pisces is mystical, ethereal, and also kind. Although she is difficult—some may even say impossible—to contain (the ocean is infinite, after all), Venus loves dwelling in this romantic sign. In fact, Venus is "exalted" in this sign, meaning that it functions at its highest vibration when in Pisces. Venus in Pisces finds beauty in everything. This partner is particularly drawn to creative pursuits, such as music and art, as well as spirituality. Venus in Pisces also has a siren-like energy: its enchanting quality can definitely throw suitors overboard and into its depths.

Mars in Pisces

Mars is aggressive, while Pisces is a true pacifist. Accordingly, when Mars enters this sign, its volatility is extinguished by Pisces's gentle waves. Mars is no longer motivated by force; instead, it's inspired by clairvoyance. In this psychic placement, Mars in Pisces is guided by intuition. It's important for her to explore her magical gifts (both in and out of the bedroom), and she often uses sex as a spiritual language. Just as the Pisces's glyph depicts two fish attached by an invisible string, for this sensitive soul, intimacy creates a powerful bond, linking her with her lover for all eternity.

Index

About the Author

Elaine Dawn is an astrologer dedicated to sharing her unique insights into the stars with clients from all walks of life.